10 SIMPLE THINGS YOU CAN DO NOW TO PROFOUNDLY CHANGE THE WORLD

HELEN MCCONNELL

WORLD OF WONDER
PUBLISHING

PORTLAND, OREGON

Cover and interior design by Julie Melfi, Leg Up Creative.

MEDICAL DISCLAIMER: The author of this book does not dispense medical advice or prescribe the use of any technique as a form of treatment for physical, emotional, or medical problems without the advice of a physician, psychologist, psychiatrist or other licensed health care professional, either directly or indirectly. The intent of the author is only to offer information of a general nature to help you in your quest for emotional and spiritual wellbeing. In the event you use any of the information in this book for yourself, the author assumes no responsibility for your actions. Any application of the material set forth in the following pages is at the reader's discretion and his or her sole responsibility.

1st edition, September 2017
ISBN-8: 978-1976385797
ISBN-10: 1976385792

Credits for Illustration:

Introduction: Tapping Chart by Shirley Gibbons

"Imagine all the people living life in peace.
You may say that I'm a dreamer,
but I'm not the only one.
I hope someday you'll join us,
and the world will be as one."

~John Lennon

CONTENTS

Introduction. . . . . *vii*

Acknowledgements. . . . . *xxiii*

#1 Stop Judging Yourself. Start Appreciating Yourself....1

#2 Stop Judging Others. Start Appreciating Others. . . .21

#3 Clear Your Clutter 33

#4 Focus on What You're For (Law of Attraction). 43

#5 Have Fun!. 57

#6 Cultivate a Positive Mind. 73

#7 Discover Your Unique Gifts. 89

#8 Heal Yourself. 107

#9 Take 100% Responsibility for Your Own Life. 131

#10 Know Your Values...and Your Value!. 149

INTRODUCTION

Do you ever feel hopeless about the state of the world? Do you ever feel like there are so many problems and not enough solutions? Do you feel overwhelmed, and so you don't really do anything about the problems?

You're not alone. Anxiety and overwhelm and stress are at all-time highs. People feel traumatized by the news. Fear is at the root of these negative emotions. But what can one person do? How can one person have an impact on the planet and Humanity? These are the questions I used to ask myself.

For most of my life I felt powerless. I wanted to help relieve the suffering that I saw in the world. I wanted to ease people's pain. But I was suffering, I was in pain. One day I had an epiphany. I'm sure it's not original to me, but it was the first time I had had this revelation. I suddenly knew that if I wanted to have an impact on Humanity and the world, the best way to help others is to help myself first.

In this book, you will discover 10 simple things you can do to profoundly change the world. I urge you to try some or all of them and see what happens to your inner and outer worlds. You are way more powerful than you realize! Each of the Ten Simple Steps is a practice in "inner work," to find your personal power and well-being. And "practice" is the key. You may notice immediate shifts, or it may take time. I encourage you to take up the practice. The world needs you!

During the many years that I was an alcoholic and a drug addict, there wasn't much I could do to help anyone else - I was way too involved in my own addictions. I know for a fact that there were people who wanted me to stop drinking and using drugs, and many of them judged me or felt sorry for me, were afraid for me, felt powerless. But judgement and pity and fear were the last things I needed to get a grip on my problem. Compassion, understanding, and a solution - that's what finally got me out of the dark and into the light.

As I began my personal and spiritual healing journey over 30 years ago, I discovered that I was powerless over most things that I had previously tried to "fix" or "control". I was powerless over all the events and reactions "out there." I was powerless over people, places, and things. But I wasn't (and I had this backwards for most of my life) powerless over my own thoughts, feelings, and reactions. I had thought that when it came to me, "That was just the way it was. I was just the way I was. And when they started acting better, I'd feel better."
I actually feel grateful for my learning experiences. I'm grateful I was an alcoholic and a drug addict. I'm grateful for all the things I didn't learn until I was in my fifties. I'm grateful for who I truly am, and for the fact that it took me over 50 years to begin to remove the trappings behind which I had hidden all those years. All of these experiences have made me a better practitioner and teacher. All these experiences have opened my eyes and my heart to compassion and what it really means. I am more inspired than ever to share a message of hope and self-empowerment and healing and connection.

As a child, I saw an angel. She used to visit me as I dozed off to sleep or just as I was waking. I called her "the light girl," but now I realize she was an angel. She is always with me still, but I can't see her with my eyes anymore. I see her with my heart.

When I was 11 and 12, growing up in Kailua, my family was not at all religious, but I wanted to go to church. I liked the music, and I wanted to feel something. I didn't know then what I was searching for. On Sundays, I would walk to the neighborhood church and attend the "grownup" service in the sanctuary. At 13 and 14, my friend Virginia's father was a minister in another church in Kailua, so I started going there. Virginia was and is one of the funniest people I know, and she and I would giggle through the service. I couldn't believe that she didn't get in trouble from her dad. But Pastor Warren was the real deal - a loving Christian man. They were few and far between. I always felt a little uncomfortable around him - like he could see through my bullshit. Like he knew that I was doing stuff during the week that didn't align with the message he was preaching. But I know now that I was feeling my own self-judgement, out of alignment with my deeply hidden spiritual self. He wasn't judging me and neither was God.

I started drinking alcohol when I was 14. By age 16, I was an alcoholic. I went to school, I had a job, but I drank at every opportunity, and I drank to get drunk, to escape how it felt to live in my skin. I drank alcoholically whenever I could, until just before my 30th birthday.

What I'd been searching for all those years wasn't "out there", it was in here, in my heart and soul. I hadn't been searching for religion, I had been searching for God. I was searching for self-acceptance. I was searching for self-love. On October 30, 1987, I experienced God in a big way - at my first AA meeting. There were about 1000 sober alcoholics in the room that night. It was an AA conference in Honolulu. I laughed, I cried, I felt like I had surrendered. When I went to my car that night, I looked up and said, "Thank you, God!" I had never said those words before. And I've never had a drink or used drugs since.

Later, in 1990, I gave birth to a miracle - my daughter, Lillian. In that moment I experienced unconditional love. In 1992, 1994, and 1996 respectively, Genevieve, Maggie, and Jeffrey were born. I was truly blessed. These powerful souls had chosen me to be their mother. What an honor! I learned about personal power and advocacy and letting go and trust and love from those children. I learned that every person is truly unique and individual - even when they have the same parents. Those children have all grown into amazing young adults.

And now I am in the midst of answering the most profound calling of my life. Throughout this book I offer exercises and Tapping protocols. Tapping (a form of EFT, Emotional Freedom Techniques) came to me when I was once again searching. It is a profound healing technique that is both simple and complex. Tapping is personal, portable, powerful and permanent. Tapping works on any emotional issue, which as humans means everything. Every action, every thought, every experience we have involves emotions - whether we're aware of them or not! Tapping is the ideal technique because you can do the work yourself or with a practitioner. It is so simple to learn and use. There are no known negative side effects. You can teach it to a 2 year old or a 92 year old. You can take it with you wherever you go. It crosses all barriers of language, religion, gender and sexual orientation, and culture, because, although I've given "scripts" for you to use, Tapping does not require the use of words. It works brilliantly in silence, too. And we all have the same emotions! We simply have different stories and experiences.

Tapping and I fell in love at first sight, and we've been devoted partners ever since. I personally began having these amazing healing moments using this simple technique. I began to get to the deep dark "shadow side" of myself, in a way I never dreamed possible. The freedom I felt, and continue to feel, as I began to heal was profound. On my own, and with the help of other Tapping practitioners, I resolved my deepest traumas, I dissipated the deep pool of shame that I swam in most of my life, discovering that at its roots, my shame wasn't even my own - I had inherited it as if it were an emotional family heirloom. I gained self-esteem. I found myself. I gained, and continue to gain, a deeper connection with the Divine. Tapping takes me way beyond what anything has before.

In my early days of Tapping, I was working at a job that I didn't like. I worked with many people, particularly a man who could be verbally abusive - not just to me. I decided to try Tapping on my feelings about this person and his behavior. When I got to a place of inner calm and acceptance of him, I discovered that he never abused me again. Whether anyone else noticed the change, I can't say. But it was profound for me. And it was in that experience that I realized that we really do affect those around us with the energy of our being.

I had never said a word to this person about their behavior towards me, and the behavior changed because my perception changed. I knew then the power of Tapping. No, it's not magic, although the results seem magical. It's a powerful energy technique. And we are made up of energy. Our thoughts, emotions, and beliefs are energetic in nature.

I figured that if I could use Tapping to make myself feel better, and in doing that, seemingly affect others, I needed to teach this to as many people as possible. Over the years since then, that is what I have done and continue to do. And that is the intention of this book - to open up the minds of as many people as possible to the power of inner change work and love. The power to change ourselves and Humanity and the planet.

Tapping is not meant to replace medical protocols or treatments. By using the protocols in this book, you agree to the disclaimer located inside the front cover of this book.

TAPPING BASICS

So you've heard about this weird thing called Tapping and you want to learn more. Maybe you've seen people doing it. Maybe you've tried it yourself or with someone else, and you want to find out more about it. How can something so simple be so powerful?

Welcome! You are joining with millions of people on the planet who are already taking advantage of the healing modality that you carry with you at all times, Tapping (which is also known as EFT or Emotional Freedom Techniques), was developed by Gary Craig, a Stanford-trained engineer. Gary learned Thought Field Therapy (TFT) from the late Dr. Roger Callahan, an American psychologist, and Dr. Callahan developed TFT using acupressure meridian points and tapping on them in different ways to address different symptoms in his clinical patients.

When something frightens us, the "Fight or Flight" response (which originates in the Amygdala portion of the brain) is "switched on." This response is for basic survival, and the body responds by creating Cortisol (a stress hormone), and delivering it to the bloodstream, increasing heart rate, shutting down the immune system, sending blood away from the brain and to the extremities - all in preparation to run for your life, or fight for your life or "freeze" (play dead). This is great if you're being chased by a tiger, or are about to step in front of a moving bus, or if you are actually being attacked. The problem for modern humans is that our response to things like someone cutting us off on the freeway, or the boss calling us into the office, or our partner forgetting to take the garbage out, feel like an attack, and have the same intense response.

The Fight or Flight response is "on" most of the time for most people in Western Cultures. The response doesn't turn off because our thoughts keep repeating what might have happened, or what actually happened but isn't now happening. The effect on our health is devastating. The cause of 90% of illness, dis-ease, and pain is "stress" - a physical response to thoughts and emotions.

Tapping calms the body's nervous system, and "turns off" the "Fight or Flight" response.

Although the results from Tapping have always been quite profound, the original evidence for the efficacy of Tapping was mostly anecdotal. But in the past 10 years, a mounting body of scientific, data-based, objective, unbiased, repeatable evidence has been documented. In fact, for a technique like Tapping that is outside the mainstream, additional evidence has been required to gain the approval of its use/efficacy by the American Psychological Association (APA). The APA finally gave EFT (Tapping) its approval for CE credits

)16, after numerous requests by ACEP (Association for Comprehensive Energy Psychology).

Now we have scientific evidence to back up what we've known for over 30 years: Tapping works! Tapping calms the Fight or Flight response, the nervous system is thus relaxed, and from this state, emotions can be "completed," and released from the body. We've also discovered that Tapping works exceptionally well for treating past traumatic events from the, and for clearing epigenetic responses. Cellular memories (emotions that are passed down from generation to generation) are powerful targets for Tapping.

As old emotions and "stuck" energy are released, the body is free to create new dreams, new responses, and new beliefs about the world. These changes have the potential to change everything.

Isn't it time to for you to experience emotional freedom? Tapping is just the tool for the job!

**For more on the scientific research studies, reports, outcome studies, review articles, skeptical and opposing viewpoints, and more, go here:

http://www.eftuniverse.com/research-studies/eft-research

Here are just a few of the things I have used Tapping for - for myself and with clients:

- Chronic pain
- Sleep disorders
- Headache
- Tension
- Anxious feelings
- Relationship issues of all kinds
- Self esteem problems
- Forgiveness
- Intense emotions and emotional reactions - like anger, frustration, rage
- Shame and guilt
- Feeling depressed
- Healing of traumatic memories, including PTSD
- Self-sabotage issues
- Money issues
- Clearing clutter
- Test anxiety
- Fears and phobias
- Cravings
- Sexual dysfunction
- Traumatic memories
- Traumatic Stress
- Intimacy issues
- And more. So much more!

You may think that Tapping on lost car keys is a joke. But think about it. When you can't find your car keys and you're on the way out the door, what is your response? If you get stressed and the voice in your head berates you for being unorganized or wasting time, you are in that Fight or Flight response. You don't have the brainpower to calmly remember where you left your keys. But Tapping will calm you down and essentially allow your subconscious mind to remind you where you left your keys. I invite you to learn Tapping and try it on everything.

Cautionary note.

When Tapping with others, I suggest you avoid Tapping with those closest to you. Because we're dealing with emotions and emotional issues, loved ones' issues are likely to trigger our own issues. At this point, it becomes difficult to maintain focus and objectivity. That's a no-win situation. And until you've done a lot of Tapping on your own issues, it will be virtually impossible for you to maintain neutrality about your loved-ones' issues.

Who Can Use Tapping?

Tapping has been used on people of all ages, around the world. Even small children can use to learn to use Tapping. Adjust the phrasing to suit the age of a small child. For example, instead of saying "I love and accept myself," use a more age-appropriate phrase like, "I'm a great kid anyway," or "I know my parents love me," or something that is true for them.

You're never too old for Tapping. It doesn't matter how long you've had a particular feeling, belief, traumatic memory, etc., Tapping can help you get to emotional freedom.

Tapping has been used in Rwanda, to help genocide survivors heal from their traumatic memories, and go on to live productive lives. https://www.createglobalhealing.org/programs/project-light-rwanda/

Tapping is now being used in some schools to help kids feel comfortable and safe, to build self-esteem, to lower test anxiety, and more. The results are happier students and teachers, improved grades, reduced bullying, increased compassion, and more.

HOW TO DO TAPPING - THE BASIC PROTOCOL

Tapping is a very simple, yet very powerful healing modality. It consists of tapping on specific acupressure meridian points with the fingertips, while focusing on negative emotions and expressing them in words*. Research now shows that when we gently tap on these acupressure meridian points, our body experiences a significant reduction of the stress hormone, Cortisol in a very short period of time. This is evidence that Tapping reduces stress and calms the nervous system.

Here is the "Basic Protocol".

For more information and an instructional video on how to tap, please visit my website, HelenMcConnell.com, http://HelenMcConnell.com and click on the "About" tab, then click on "Tapping."

We begin by tapping gently on the **side of the hand**, which is the soft, fleshy part of the side of the hand - between the wrist and the finger joint. You can use two or three or four fingertips to tap the right hand with the left hand or the left hand with the right hand - it doesn't matter. You can switch hands while tapping.

Tapping is done in a gentle manner - there's no need to "pound." There is no set number of taps per point. 6 or 7 taps is fine. More is okay.

Next, we tap on the **crown of the head**, using the fingertips, and gently tapping the top, center of the head. You can tap in a small circle, or spread your fingers to include both sides of the skull/brain.

Then we move to the **inner eyebrow point**. This is the inside edge of the eyebrow - left side, right side, or both sides simultaneously - whichever feels right for you.

The **outer eye** is the next spot - tapping gently on the outer corner of one eye or both - again, whatever feels right to you.

Move to the **under-eye point** - directly below the mid-pupil if you're looking straight ahead. There is a bone right below your eye - that is the place to tap. Often people end up tapping on their cheek. Don't worry if this happens - Tapping will still work. You can tap on one or both under-eye points.

Then the **under-nose point** is tapped. We tap in that little indent directly below the nose and above the upper lip.

The next spot is called the **chin point**, but is actually located above the chin and below the lower lip, in the indent.

The **collarbone points** are next. Find your collar bones with your fingers. Then move down about an inch and out about an inch from your collarbones. There is a soft spot that is often tender. Tap here. Tap on one or the other or both. I often reach my full hand across from one collarbone point to the other, and including my heart chakra.

And the final point in the Basic Protocol is the **underarm point**. You can tap one or the other, or both. Reach across your chest to the opposite side of your body, under your arm. The Tapping point is about 4 inches down from your armpit - on the bra line or nipple line. You may also choose to reach up under your arm, "monkey style" to tap on the underarm point or points.

These 9 points make up **"a round" of Tapping**.

Now to add words and phrases by creating a "setup statement," and "reminder phrases." First, determine what you want to Tap on? Are you angry? In pain? Frustrated? Do you have low self-esteem? Notice what's bugging you. Pick ONE thing at a time to Tap on. This "one thing" is your "Tapping Target." Say it or write it down in a sentence. For example, "I'm angry at my boss for not appreciating me."

Notice where you FEEL the anger in your body. In other words, how do you know it's anger and not happiness. There are distinct sensations in the body which tell you what you're feeling. You may not be used to noticing these feelings. In fact, you may have spent most of your life trying NOT to feel them. But they're there. If you can't find the sensation yet, don't worry. You can still tap.

Rate the intensity of the feeling, using a Subjective scale of 0-10, with 10 being the most intense. You can't get this answer wrong, and it is for measurement only.

Once you determine your "Tapping Target" (whatever is bugging you), begin by Tapping on the Side of the Hand Point while saying something like, "Even though I feel anger because my boss doesn't appreciate me [fill in with your own emotion or concern], I deeply and completely love and accept myself." This is the "Setup Statement" and can be adjusted to suit your situation. However, the comment about accepting myself is an important part of Tapping.

Now, while still tapping on the Side of the Hand Point, say something like, "Even though I feel this anger in my chest. And I feel it at an intensity of 8, I love and accept myself."

And once more, while still tapping on the Side of the Hand Point, say something like, "Even though I have this anger feeling in my chest, I love and accept myself."

That is the Setup Statement part of the Tapping Basic Recipe.

Begin at the top of the head point, and say a short "reminder phrase" that harks back to your Setup Statement. Say one reminder phrase as you tap at each point. Something like this:
(Top of head point) "This anger,"
(Inner eyebrow point) "I feel this anger at my boss,"
(Side of eye point) "My boss doesn't appreciate me,"
(Under eye point) "I feel this anger at an 8,"
(Under nose point) "This anger,"
(Chin point) "I feel this anger,"
(Collarbone point) "I feel this anger at my boss,"
(Under arm point) "This anger."

Then take a deep, cleansing breath, in and out. Then sense in again at your anger. Notice where you felt it before and how intense it was. Is it still the same? Does it feel the same? Is it the same intensity?

Make a note of any changes, and tap again. This time, your Setup Statement will be something like this: "Even though I have this remaining anger, I love and accept myself," and following the above instructions.

Continue to tap until the intensity of your anger (or whatever you're tapping on) drops to a 3 or lower. If the intensity doesn't drop after 3 or 4 rounds of Tapping, check your Setup Statement for specificity. If the statement is too general, the intensity may go down slowly and not so noticeably.

A Few More Tips About Tapping.

- You can't get it wrong. Just do it. That's the most important thing to know.
- Don't worry about what to say. Just say your truth. The Tapping Basic Recipe was developed for the best

results, and we have discovered that even if you don't use the "correct" Setup Statement, Tapping will still work.

- You won't hurt yourself
- Even very young kids can tap!
- You can tap (very gently) on babies and on pets. Sometimes babies or pets are super-sensitive to
- Tapping and don't really like it. In this case, gently touch and hold each Tapping point, or softly
- stimulate the points by briefly moving your fingers in a circular motion on each one. Or you can surrogately tap on yourself on behalf of a pet or baby.

Please note: You can Tap on the Tapping points (meridian points) anytime, without using any words. Your subconscious mind is always "thinking," and Tapping works on much more than you're aware of. So tap, even if you "don't know what to say."

Here's a Tapping Points chart for your reference.

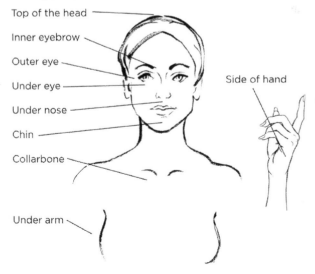

Top of the head
Inner eyebrow
Outer eye
Under eye
Under nose
Chin
Collarbone
Side of hand
Under arm

For more details and a free downloadable PDF, please visit HelenMcConnell.com.

ACKNOWLEDGEMENTS

I offer my heartfelt gratitude to those who directly influenced this book.

Dawn Murray for always encouraging me and helping me to find myself and my own unique voice.

ToiAnn Hanson for taking me step-by-step through the book-writing process, and for all the other support and encouragement you've offered.

Julie Melfi for creating an inspiring cover, typesetting the book, and for going above and beyond to get this book published, for getting my new website up and running, and for keeping me on track.

Anne Hawley, for sharing her experience as a published author, and for all the other support you've offered me.

Elena Maltais for being a wonderful combination of friend, supporter, colleague, and fan.

Marilyn McWilliams for always reminding me that it's okay to do it my way.

Kris Bradley for some amazing insights, lots of encouragement, and being a wonderful friend!

#1 STOP JUDGING YOURSELF. START APPRECIATING YOURSELF

"You express your own divinity by being alive and by loving yourself and others."

~Miguel Ruiz

WHO IS JUDGING YOU?

You are, most likely, your own worst critic. You learned to judge yourself at an early age, from others who judged you and themselves. It felt so bad when they judged you that you learned to do it to yourself before someone else did it to you, in an effort to avoid the pain of being judged by someone else again. And you believed the criticism because you were too young to think for yourself, and you trusted whoever was judging you.

Then it became a habit - to judge yourself and criticize yourself. And here you are, wondering why you doubt yourself or sabotage yourself, or why you don't have better regard for yourself. You may be wondering why you don't get the respect you deserve or make the money you want. It has been you who taught the world how to treat you. You've been saying these negative things to yourself nearly your whole life. And you've been listening!

It may seem like a quiet critical voice in the back of your mind, so you don't think your self-judgment is that bad. But it's those quiet little voices that are like recorded loops - saying the same things over and over. And those things aren't very nice. Imagine your 4-year-old self hearing you saying to her "You're so stupid!" or "What is wrong with you?" or You've always been fat!" or any of a variety of other things that essentially translate into "You're not good enough, and I don't like you." How do you think your 4-year-old self feels? Go ahead and ask her. Is that how you want to raise yourself?

There may be a louder voice that is constantly belittling you and chastising you. It might be more obvious that it's happening, but you haven't stopped it yet. Only you can stop self-judgment.

Whether you're aware of all the times you judge yourself or not, it is happening at a subconscious level more than at a conscious level. You can prove this by asking yourself, "Do I consciously choose to say those things to myself? Or do they seem to come out on their own - out of habit, and without any thought?" If you do consciously choose to judge yourself and be harsh, you need to stop. Because you are abusing yourself, and your 4-year-old self. You need to be her advocate. And your own. If you're not choosing to say those things, which is much more likely, you need to become aware when you say them and stop. And then you need to break that habit. Not only for you, but for all of Humanity.

You may be wondering, "Why would self-judgment have any impact on the world, let alone a profound impact?" Here are three reasons:

Reason #1: If you're judging yourself and not accepting yourself, you are basically saying that you don't think you are good enough, and that who you really are needs to be hidden away. Hiding your true self away is a lot of work and takes tremendous energy. Energy that you could be using for something important!

Reason #2: The best way to impact and profoundly change the world, to impact and profoundly change Humanity, is to find your greatest gifts and use them and share them. Everyone, absolutely everyone has a gift. It's there in your Soul, waiting for you to uncover it and bring it forth. And then to go out and encourage others to do the same. In this way you can begin to fulfill yourself and fulfill your Soul's destiny.

Most of us hide our greatest gifts behind fear - usually fear of being judged. Most of us are afraid to be truly great. And many of us have never had an inkling of our own expansiveness. We've been telling ourselves we're not good enough, we're not loveable for so long that we can't see the evidence to the contrary, even when it's right in our face.

Reason #3: You must take care of yourself before you can truly take care of anyone else, and self-acceptance is the place to begin to care for yourself. Self-acceptance is the antithesis of self-judgment. It is the beginning of all healing. If you're judging yourself, there's a very good chance you're judging others as well.

If you belittle and berate yourself, you are abandoning yourself. We are "listening" continually to our own dysfunctional mental commentary. We are harming ourselves emotionally, physically, and spiritually with our own negativity. It's time to stop.

Our subconscious thoughts are way more powerful than our conscious thoughts because we have so many more subconscious thoughts than conscious ones. Our subconscious mind never stops "thinking" - not even when we sleep. So if our predominant subconscious thoughts are critical and judgmental, we are continually cutting ourselves down, beating ourselves up, demoralizing ourselves, letting ourselves down.

If you are judging yourself - with your thoughts, your words, and your actions, then you are depriving yourself and the world of your greatest gifts. You are depriving yourself of joy and happiness and fulfillment. You are depriving yourself of the feeling of oneness with Humanity and God/the Universe/the Divine Creator/Allah/Holy Spirit.

Think about it - who would you be if you showed up really big in the world, sharing your gifts, braving criticism, breaking molds, shifting paradigms? Does that thought excite you? Scare you? Both? When you discover your gifts, you just know what you need to do to truly shine and to share them in a way that benefits yourself and others. That is true greatness. If you're not doing that, self-judgment and fear of judgment by others is the only thing keeping you from that greatness.

Imagine if every person you know was to find their own unique gifts and begin to share them in the world in their own unique ways. There would be people who are healers, some who are caretakers, some would sit with the dying, others would play with the children, there would be many exceptional cooks, there would be scientists, a bunch of them would find a new source for energy, a group of people would end homelessness in your community, some would make sure that kids stay off drugs, many would help others to get off the drugs they're already on. There would be a bunch of people who would improve working conditions. Another group would develop technology to make lives easier.

There would be farmers. Some people would drive buses. Yes, there really are people for whom driving a bus is their gift. They are friendly to the passengers, they are safe drivers, courteous. And they enjoy their work. There would be people who keep the streets clean and take away garbage, not because it's the only job they could get, but because they really want to.

There would be people who seemingly don't do anything. But they would be encouraged to keep searching for their gifts, and then to share them. Not with guilt or shame or judgment, but with compassion and love and encouragement. There would be actors and singers and poets and playwrights. There would be boat builders and car washers, building builders and dog washers. And there would be people who bring forth gifts like we've never before seen.

Besides sharing their gifts, each of these people would feel fulfilled by their work. There would be very little to complain about, and lots to appreciate. People would spend their time dreaming and imagining even greater things, rather than moping around abusing themselves. Compassion would be rampant. There would be unrestrained caring for others. Every day you would see people rising to their higher potential, rather than sinking to their limitations.

That would be profound! Let it begin with me and you!

LIFE FORCE ENERGY

There is an energy keeping each of us alive. It's called Life Force. This energy is all around us and through us. It is the force that keeps our skin cells together so that the rest of us can be us. Life Force keeps our lungs breathing and our heart beating and our cells reproducing. It is also the force that keeps the Earth spinning on its axis, and keeps the planets revolving around the sun. Life Force energy is benevolent. It is infinite. It is creative. Life Force energy is Divinity itself. It is God.

Life Force flows through us through our nervous system. Ideally, unrestricted flow of Life Force creates vibrant health in our bodies and in all things. Critical thoughts cause our Life-Force energy to constrict. You know when you feel stressed you feel constricted? It's because you are constricted. Constricting Life-Force is constricting vibrant health. You can eat all organic food, drink healthy protein smoothies, exercise every day, and stay hydrated...but if your predominant thoughts are negative - about yourself or others - you are going to begin to notice a breakdown of your physical self.

Isn't self-appreciation conceited?

Having a high self-regard is not conceited. Having self-confidence is not arrogant. When we truly love ourselves, we are honoring the Divine because we are the physical manifestation of the Divine. If you want to make the most of your life, you've got to encourage yourself to BE yourself, have confidence in yourself, keep yourself free from criticism. Whether the criticism comes from you or from someone else, and is about you, or whether it comes from you and is about others, it will harm you. You see, your body and your mind don't know the difference between "self-judgment" and "other-judgment." The energy is the same. Regarding yourself with deep love and respect is in alignment with the Divine and allows Life Force to flow through you unrestricted. This is the single best way to gain vibrant health. And to find and use your gifts.

BE *FOR* YOURSELF!

In keeping with the themes of this book, I'm going to encourage you to focus on what you're FOR, rather than focusing on what you're against. Start with yourself. Starting right now, begin to encourage yourself, to love yourself, to forgive yourself - rather than "not judging" yourself. Let's start by wording it in that positive way.

Now that you know that self-criticism is hurting you, why would you continue to do it? You don't have a choice, that's why. Not until you decide to take back your thinking, and begin to master your mind. The key here is deciding. Decide right now to become a more conscious thinker. Decide right now to learn to change your subconscious thought patterns. And decide to stop judging yourself.

And once you decide, you've got to practice because these critical thoughts and beliefs are so deeply conditioned into you. It's going to take close monitoring of your thoughts and emotions to notice, and then redirect your thinking, until new neural pathways are created in your brain. Tapping is great for this very "neuronal pathway creation!"

WHY DOES IT MATTER?

Why does how you talk to yourself in your head have anything to do with changing the world?

If you are judging yourself, you are holding yourself back from being the greatest version of you. If you are holding yourself back from being the greatest version of you then the world is suffering. When you begin to become the greatest version of you, the world is profoundly affected, one ripple at a time. As you encourage yourself, you'll find yourself encouraging others. And there's a chance that they will feel better about themselves and begin to become better versions of themselves. They will be nicer and kinder and more encouraging to others, and things will really begin to change for the better. This amazing change is already happening around the globe. If you haven't noticed it, then you are still criticizing yourself.

THOUGHTS BECOME THINGS

What you think about becomes reality. What you put your attention to grows, expands, increases. What most people don't realize is that our thoughts occur mostly at a subconscious level. It has been researched and determined that about 90% or more of our thoughts each day are subconscious, which means we're not choosing most of what we're thinking. Those thoughts are "programmed" into us, mostly from an early age. We are patterned beings living mostly patterned lies.

Do you ever wonder why the same types of things keep happening in your life? Do you ever think "here we go again"? Or say "That's the story of my life!"? Or maybe you haven't given it much thought. You might just think it's your lot in life. But it's not. It's your subconscious thinking. And that can be changed.

Recently I was working with a woman who belongs to a Tapping Group I facilitate each week, so we've worked together many times. But it wasn't until today that she began to realize that she has a "belief" that "People will always clean up my messes." This came from early childhood when her father would see crumbs under the table while the kids were eating and yell at them about the mess. And then the father would clean it up. This seems like such a seemingly innocent kind of thing, but to a child, when an event like this happens over and over, she unconsciously "decides" that she makes messes and someone else cleans them up. She was quickly able to see how this has been a "theme" in her life. Not always with food under the table, but with all kinds of messes and unfinished stuff. Yes, she went to college and had a career, but her deeper calling is in service as a teacher and mentor to help empower girls and young women. She would like to take her business to a new level, but was afraid of the responsibility. You see, with the belief that "someone else will clean up my messes," she never really learned to be joyously responsible for herself. Together, we used Tapping to release this belief from her nervous system, and freed her to begin allowing her business to flourish.

DEVELOPING NEW THINKING PATTERNS

Read on to find out some simple ways to begin to change your subconscious thought patterns. This is such an important idea and protocol that I've repeated it several times in this book.

Remember when you first learned how to drive a car (or ride a bike, or roller blade)? You had to think about every little step: Unlocking the doors, opening the driver's door, sliding in behind the wheel, putting on the seatbelt, putting the key in the ignition and starting the engine, adjusting the mirrors, taking off the parking brake, using the turn signal, pushing the gas pedal, pushing the brake pedal, and every little thing about driving.

But after just a few practice drives, most of that had become automatic. You now know how to drive without really thinking about it. When you get in your car, do you have to stop and figure out how to unlock the doors? Or how to open the door? Or how to slide in behind the steering wheel and put on your seat belt? When you were first driving you did. That's when you were using your conscious mind to drive.

But now it's become habit, and you don't have to give it much thought. And that's a good thing. That's your subconscious mind at work. When you go to drive a friend's car or a rental car, you'll need to use your conscious mind again for a little while. But soon you'll again be driving without really thinking.

You learned how to judge yourself when you were very, very young. Someone else (usually parents, older siblings, and teachers) taught you. At first, it felt strange and awkward to you to be so mean to yourself. You may not remember that. Your subconscious mind remembers, though. It records everything you've ever experienced - every sight, smell, sound, every emotion, every hurt - and stores those memories away.

Those people around you learned how to judge from their parents, older siblings, and teachers. judgment may have come with words, such as, "Why are you so loud?" "You're too quiet!" "Why can't you be like your brother?" "What is wrong with you?" "You are such an idiot!" "You'll never amount to anything," or worse! The judgment you experienced may have been non-verbal - that look your mother always gave you, or the silent treatment you got from your father when he was disappointed in you - or you may have suffered physical abuse. Your self-judgment may have come when someone humiliated you - maybe a teacher called on you and you didn't know the answer and the class laughed at you. And if you were ever hit, slapped, spanked, or endured any other physical abuse, the judgment got embedded and more deeply embedded with each occurrence.

At first, the judgment may have come from others, but soon you learned to judge yourself. Almost as if you felt the need to judge yourself before anyone else got the chance. Or you figured that self-judgment was the way to fit in with your family. Whatever the case, it was your subconscious mind protecting you. This became your

However you learned it, self-judgment has been your constant companion, whether you're aware of it or not. That's your subconscious mind at work.

When we judge ourselves, we immediately put limitations on ourselves - what we can do or be. When we judge others, we put limitations on our own reality - what they can do or be. We become self-identified with our thinking when our thoughts are happening to us and we're believing them. It's as if our thoughts are thinking US!

We each see the world through our own internal "filters." These filters are created throughout our lives by parents, siblings, teachers, peers, media, religious affiliations, cultural affiliations, and our own personal experiences. In this way, we create our reality. Understanding this can help us change our reality.

THERE IS HOPE!

We each have the capacity to create a greater reality for ourselves. When you stop judging yourself, which at first takes a conscious effort, your reality will change and expand - usually dramatically!

You might be asking, "What does it mean to "change my reality?" Good question. Let me describe what it doesn't mean. When you change your reality, you won't wake up in someone else's house. Your friends will still recognize you (though some of them may fade out of your life). You won't be shape-shifting. But the world in which you live will seem different.

Try these simple exercises to learn to stop judging yourself, and begin to create profound change in the world:

EXERCISE #1 to begin to stop judging yourself.
- Stop for a few minutes and sit still. Breathe deeply and relax. Relax further, but don't go to sleep.
- Mentally scan your body slowly from head to toe. Notice any tension that resides there, and use your mind to focus on the tension - asking it to relax. This isn't about perfection. This is about becoming aware of your mind and your body, and beginning to see how they work together.
- Now simply "check-in" with your mind and body, and sense the ways you judge yourself: your body, your mind, your characteristics, your nature, the way you live your life, your success.

- Breathe deeply again as you notice that you are harsh with yourself sometimes. Maybe you're harsh with yourself often.

"As I let go of self-judgement, I find it easier to let go of all judgement."

- Become aware of what you're thinking. Or rather, what's programmed in you that's thinking YOU.
- Write down some of the phrases you think about yourself and say about yourself. Be honest and thorough. Don't sugar-coat the words. It's important that you examine this.
- Now look at those words and phrases. Ask yourself how it makes you feel to say those things to yourself. Really notice if you feel energized, or depleted. Do you feel loved, or judged? Do you feel stronger, or weaker?
- If someone else said these things to you, how would you feel?
- Did someone else ever say these things to you? Where did you learn to say them to yourself?

Most of my clients tell me that if they are hard on themselves and judge themselves, they think they will be motivated to do more, and to BE more. But this just isn't true. [If you wanted to climb a mountain, would it be more helpful for you to have someone behind you yelling, "You're an idiot! A weakling! You'll never get up this mountain!"? Or would you respond better to someone behind you saying "You can do this! I'm here with you to encourage you and to support you.

And climbing this mountain is just the beginning of what we'll accomplish together! You rock!" Your inner voice can be either of these voices.

You learned how to judge yourself (and how to judge others) when you were very young. No one said "you should judge yourself, and you should look at others and judge them." But rather, the important people in your life when you were young "taught" you by example. THEY judged themselves. THEY judged others. And THEY judged YOU. THEY learned it when THEY were a kid. It's not their fault. It's not your fault. No one is to blame.

I have included Tapping in every chapter of this book, because for me, Tapping has been the most powerful tool I have ever experienced to release old limiting beliefs and allow my authentic self to come through. Read more about Tapping in the Introduction.

Here is some Tapping that can help with overcoming self-judgement, and begin self-appreciation.

First, begin with some self-forgiveness Tapping. I have loosely adapted the Hawaiian self-forgiveness technique called Ho'o ponopono (pronounced Ho-oh-po-no-po-no). I often share this in group tapping classes as well as individual sessions. The effects are quite profound.

Tapping around the points, beginning at the top of the head (we won't use the side of the hand point for this protocol), say one phrase at each point:

(Top of head) I'm so sorry, [say your own name] that I have been judging you so harshly

(Inner eyebrow) Please forgive me, [say your own name] for judging you so harshly

(Outer eye) Thank you for forgiving me, [say your own name]

(Under eye) I love you, [say your own name]

(Under nose) I'm sorry, [say your own name]

(Chin) Please forgive me, [say your own name]

(Collarbone) Thank you, [say your own name]

(Under arm) I love you, [say your own name]

Take a slow, deep breath.. Breathe in as far as you can without struggling. Don't hold your breath, but simply exhale without resistance. Take two more slow breaths in and out before moving on. Notice how your body feels. Are you feeling a bit more present? More relaxed? Your body really loves you for doing this work!

EXERCISE #2 to heal your younger self, and to begin to let go of old "stories."

What are some of the things you say to yourself about yourself? Take a moment to get clear on this. I've had clients tell me they say things to themselves like, "You're an idiot!" "You are so stupid!" "You can't do that - you didn't go to college," "What is wrong with you?" "I hate you!" "You are a lazy slob!" "God hates you!" and worse. When you begin to notice what you've been telling yourself, remember that you've been doing it way more often than you realize - probably many times per day. If your boss told you "You're an idiot!" several times a day, would you still work for that person? Would you feel motivated to do your best? Would you look forward to going to work? Of course you wouldn't!

- You're doing this to yourself and then you wonder why, at the end of the day, you feel tired and unmotivated and sluggish. You wonder why you're not more successful, why you're not making more money, why you don't feel like helping others, why you're not happy.

- Close your eyes and take a gentle, deep breath in. Begin to tap around the points. Keep tapping as you continue.

- Imagine or remember yourself as a young child - around 3 or 4 years old. Would you (the adult you) allow anyone to say those things to your young-child self - those things that you say to yourself now? I hope not!

- Let's use this moment to begin to heal, and to change the way you talk to yourself.

- Still imagining your younger self, feel your adult self getting down to her eye level, looking into her eyes, and tell her in a genuine, loving, encouraging way how sorry you are that someone called her those things.

- Tell her how sorry you are that she felt she had to believe those criticisms.

- Tell her that those things aren't true, and that she doesn't have to believe them anymore.

- Tell her that those people didn't love themselves.

- And tell her that you are learning to love yourself, and you hope she'll help you. Spend a moment in this interaction, still tapping, and really feeling yourself connect with the young version of you.

- Take a moment to find three things to really appreciate about her. Still at her eye level, tell her what you appreciate about her. If she doesn't believe you, tell her again. Convince her that it's true - she's wonderful!

Tell her in a personal way, like, "Darling, you are the most magnificent child I've ever known. You have so much love in you! I want you to know that you're never alone - i'm always here with you. I want to help you nurture your wonderful gifts - all those special things that make you YOU!"

- While still tapping, take a moment to tell her how much you love her. Let her know that she is the most important person in your life! Really feel that love in your own heart, and be sure she can feel it too.

- Watch her face as you tell her. Feel her heart as you tell her. Feel your own heart as you tell her. When she comes to believe what you're telling her, give her a big "Mama bear" hug. Embrace her fully. As you do so, integrate your young self into your own heart. Bring your hands to your heart and hold them there.

- Feel that love expanding - like swirling gold light. Feel it going through your entire body - down to your toes, into every organ in your body, up into your throat, and into your head. Now feel that love continue to expand all around you - like you're standing in a globe of that swirling gold light. Feel the globe extend out all around you - 6 inches, 12 inches, 3 feet, 6 feet.

- Invite the people you love into this golden globe, and expand it to include them.

- Now invite someone you've been angry at into the golden light. Expand the light. See how it affects them and you. Notice that there is always plenty of golden, loving light for everyone.

- Now invite all the people you don't like into the golden globe of light. See the golden light just expanding further and further around you.

- See if you can include the entire Earth in that golden light. See the Earth bathed in love. Notice how that affects all the people, the plants, the animals, the oceans, the rivers, the mountains. You are creating this image with your mind and with your love. You are creating this reality. It may only last a few seconds, but the more often you do this, the longer it will last and the more "real" it will become.

- Slowly open your eyes. See if you can continue to feel this golden loving light for 60 seconds.

- You can practice any part of this exercise with your eyes open. If you practice surrounding the Earth with your loving, golden light, it will get easier and easier, and you will really benefit.

Integration.

Using Tapping to integrate your experience, tap around the points, beginning at the top of your head, and say one phrase at each point:

(Top of head) -I've always known that I'm loved and supported
(Inner eyebrow) -I've always known that I'm not alone
(Outer eye) I've always known that I'm magnificent
(Under the eye) I've always known that I'm loved and supported
(Under nose) I've always known that I don't need to judge myself
(Chin) I've always known that I have unique gifts

(Collarbone) I've always known that I am powerful
(Under arm) I've always known that I'm loved and supported
Take a slow, deep breath in...and then exhale. Notice your feelings right now. Take some time to journal about your experience. Repeat this as often as you like.

EXERCISE #3 to begin to love your body.
Let's give some appreciation to our body. Start with a general appreciation for all your body does or has done for you. And even more powerful, thank your body for what you'd like it to do for you. Notice how you feel before you begin. And then notice how you feel after just one round of "body appreciation tapping."

Tapping around the points, beginning at the top of the head, say these phrases - one phrase at each point:

(Top of Head) Thank you, body, for everything you do for me
(Inner eyebrow) Thank you, body, for keeping my heart beating
(Outer eye) For keeping my lungs breathing
(Under eye) Thank you, body, for balancing my hormones
(Under nose) Thank you, body, for maintaining my ideal weight [even if it's not true yet, your body is listening, and will do what you tell it.]
(Chin) Thank you, body, for regulating my blood pressure
(Collarbone) Thank you, body, for giving me vibrant health
(Under arm) Thank you, body, for all the amazing things you do that I don't even know about.

Take a deep breath. Notice the energy flowing in your body. That's Life Force!

(You can add whatever phrases you want to this tapping protocol. More appreciation of your body will bring more Life Force flowing through you.)

Are you noticing any changes in your self-regard? This takes practice. Don't give up on yourself. And don't beat yourself up if you don't get it right away! Notice when you fall back into old habits, and gently nudge yourself to tap in some love and appreciation and forgiveness.

You are on your way to profoundly changing the world!

#2 STOP JUDGING OTHERS, START APPRECIATING OTHERS

"When you judge others, you do not define them, you define yourself."

~Earl Nightingale

It seems obvious that not judging others will have an impact on the world. But a profound impact? It's true. You see, everything we do, everything we say, everything we think affects ourselves and everyone else on the planet. You can't always see the impact, but it's happening, nonetheless.

When we judge others, whether or not they actually hear us, we are basically saying that they aren't good enough, that they don't live up to our expectations, that they are not Divinity.

And when we judge others, we cut off our own Life Force Energy. Your body doesn't know the difference between you judging them, and you judging you (See Chapter One).

The best ways to most profoundly affect Humanity and the planet is for each of us to do our internal work. Unless you are specifically called to be a missionary or a politician or a lawyer, then leave those issues to others. I promise you that when you do your inner work, your outer world will change. A shift in perspective is a miracle. And miracles come in all sizes.

JUDGING OTHERS SHOWS UP IN MANY WAYS

We think negative thoughts about others - about the way they look, the way they act, the way they think, how much money they make or don't make, how they live, the car they drive or don't drive, and on and on. Negative thoughts include jealousy and envy, as well as the more obvious types of "I don't like what you're doing" kind of thoughts.

We say negative things about others.

Like when you're driving in your car and someone cuts you off. You might call them a name, or swear at them, or give them the finger. You don't even know this person, and you are hurting yourself trying to get them to feel bad about what they did, or to notice how much it scared you or pissed you off. You want them to feel as bad as you do, but really, you're the one feeling bad and hanging on to feeling bad. Notice if you then get to where you're going and begin to complain about how bad the traffic was and how some person cut you off. You're continuing to feel bad by choice, and wanting other people to feel bad with you.

Exercise for judgement for when you're in the car.

Here's a quick way to take care of those moments in the car.

Take full responsibility for your own well being, and when you get upset, begin to tap. You can tap your side of the hand point against the steering wheel to stimulate that point. Tap until your anger/fear subsides.

OR: Tap like this, tapping around the points:

(Top of head) I'm sorry, [say your own name]
(Inner eyebrow) For having you think such angry thoughts
(Outer eye) I was scared and I reacted
(Under eye) Please forgive me, [say your own name]
(Under nose) Thank you for forgiving me, [say your own name]
(Chin) I love you, [say your own name]
(Collarbone) And I want the very best for you

Take a slow breath in and notice if your anger/fear has subsided. Tap again if needed. This Tapping is again loosely based on Ho'o ponopono, Hawaiian forgiveness and reconciliation technique. I've taken full liberty with this technique and added Tapping.

We gossip about others.

Gossip is judging. Gossip is repeating something seen or heard about someone else - usually without that person's permission to repeat it - with the intent of gaining something for ourselves. When we gossip about others, which is intentionally to get others to come around to our negative point of view, we hurt everyone involved. We definitely hurt the person we're gossiping about. We are purposely trying to destroy them. This is "emotional violence." We are hurting the person we're gossiping to. We have rallied them into thinking and speaking negatively. Of course, they don't need to participate, but not everyone is so enlightened that they can disengage from gossip.

We are hurting ourselves. Once again, our body doesn't know the difference between negative thoughts and words about someone else, and negative thoughts and words about our own self! So when you gossip, every cell in your body is feeling attacked. And you are hurting your environment, filling the workspace or home space or car or wherever you are with negative energy. Gossip often destroys relationships and creates distrust. I mean, do you trust a gossiper to not gossip about you?

Exercise for gossip.

Begin to notice when you gossip. Learn to catch yourself before you tell the story. Ask yourself why you want to tell this story. What is your true motive? Is it your story to tell? Do you have permission to repeat this story? Will it be helpful to all concerned for you to tell or repeat this story? If not, it's gossip!

Notice how often others gossip to you. Receiving gossip is still gossip. Find ways to interrupt gossip being given to you or from you. Change the subject, interrupt, or simply say "That's not your story to tell/not your information to share." When someone at work insists on telling everyone about the HR Director's cancer scare, that is gossip, even if it's disguised as "caring." When your mother calls to tell you about your sister's boyfriend problems, that is gossip. When you feel the need to "warn" someone that your mutual acquaintance, Mallory, isn't trustworthy, that is gossip.

Now that you've learned to notice gossip, give yourself a "no-gossip" challenge. Try one day without giving or receiving gossip. Make sure it's a day when you're around other people. Once you've accomplished a full no-gossip day, try a week. You may need to do some tapping about how difficult it feels to not gossip.

Here's a quick Tapping protocol for "quitting gossip."

Tapping around the points, say one phrase at each point, like this:

(Top of head) It's hard not to gossip!
(Inner eyebrow) I really want to share that information
(Outer eye) It's not really mine to share
(Under eye) But I still want to share it
(Under nose) It's hard not to gossip
(Chin) I like to be the first to tell
(Collarbone) And I just want to inform people
(Under arm) And save them the time and trouble

(Top of head) It's hard not to gossip!
(Inner eyebrow) I get such juicy information
(Outer eye) It's boring to not gossip
(Under eye) Gossip is entertaining
(Under nose) It's sharing
(Chin) I like to gossip!
(Collarbone) I like to be the center of attention
(Under arm) It's hard not to gossip

Take a deep breath in and out, and notice how you feel now. Did any thoughts, images, memories or insights come up for you? Is there more to tap on? You

can put your own words into that Tapping protocol. Use anything that feels right to you. But do Tap!

We complain.

Yes, complaining is judging. And it is blaming. And it is
disempowering. Complaining is a complete focus on what
we're against, with no focus on what we're FOR. Complaining
takes all the wind out of your sails. It deflates your Life Force
Energy. Complaining makes YOU the victim ("they did this
thing and I want you to know I don't like it and I can't or
won't do anything about it.") Complaining wastes your personal energy, and it sucks the energy from whomever you're
complaining to. Don't delude yourself that complaining is
feedback. They are not the same thing. Complaining is just
the same as gossiping, only is usually about the way you were
treated, while gossiping is about what someone else has done
or experienced.

When others complain to you, your Life Force Energy is
being sucked away. Either the complainer wants you to do
something about the situation, or they want you to feel bad
with them. Don't participate.

Exercises for dealing with complaining.

If YOU are the complainer: *Notice* that you complain.
Notice how often you complain - about the weather, the traffic, something that's changing, your financial situation, the
government, your boss, your clients, your customers, about
your spouse or your children or your mother or your mother-
in-law. Notice *how it feels* when you complain. Notice the
disempowering feeling. Ask yourself if you want to feel this

way more often or less often. Don't beat yourself up, but rather, own it.

Say it to yourself while tapping. Start with the side of the hand point.

Even though I'm complaining, I love and accept myself right where I am
Even though it feels disempowering, I love and accept myself right where I am
Even though I'm noticing that I complain often, I love and accept myself right where I am

Then Tapping around the points, say one phrase at each point:

(Top of head) I'm complaining
(Inner eyebrow) It feels disempowering
(Outer eye) I never noticed before how often I complain
(Under eye) I'm giving away a lot of power by complaining
(Under nose) I usually complain about things I feel powerless about
(Chin) Or things I feel are unfair
(Collarbone) But complaining isn't doing any good
(Under arm) And I'd like things to change

(Top of head) I'm not willing or able to change these situations
(Inner eyebrow) Maybe it's my perspective that needs to change
(Outer eye) Maybe my thinking needs to change
(Under eye) I do have the power to change those
(Under nose) So I give myself permission to stop complaining
(Chin) To stop disempowering myself

(Collarbone) I can choose to stop thinking about it all together (Under arm) I give myself permission to let this go

Take a deep, gentle, slow breath. You can change the wording to suit your needs, but the important thing is to get to a place of empowerment. True empowerment. Which doesn't mean violence or retribution. Nor does it mean being a doormat!

If someone is complaining to you.

Notice how often this person complains to you. If it is a rare occurrence, this person may just need someone to vent to, and you can hold space for them without getting yourself on the complaining bandwagon. You can say things like "I understand," or "I hear what you're saying," or even "How do you feel?" and "How would you rather feel?" In this way you are being compassionate, without causing yourself to suffer.

If this person often complains to you, and you notice it brings down your own energy, don't engage with the complaining. In other words, don't start complaining yourself. This will only add to the negativity, and you will both be disempowered. If this has been your pattern in the past - the two of you complaining together - you're going to need to withdraw from complaining, and possibly say something, like "I've been noticing lately how much I complain about stuff, and it feels disempowering to me. I'm working on not complaining." You're not telling them what to do or not to do, but just stating your own awareness.

Tap about how their complaining makes you feel.

Don't tap in front of them! Go into the bathroom, or go into your office, or wait until you're in your car, and tap. Here is a brief tapping routine to use:

Notice/remember how their complaining makes you feel. Do you lose energy? Do you get angry? Do you feel sad or anxious? Notice the sensations in your body. Rate the intensity of those sensations, using the 1-10 scale.

Starting on the side of the hand point, tap and say:

Even though it makes me feel anxious when they complain to me, I love and accept myself.
Even though when they complain, I find myself complaining too, and I feel anxious, I love and accept myself
Even though I don't want to listen to them complain, I don't want to be rude, and I love and accept myself

Then, Tapping around the points - say one phrase at each point:

(Top of head) They always complain to me
(Inner eyebrow) I feel anxious
(Outer eye) They always complain to me
(Under eye) And I often join in
(Under nose) I don't want to listen to them complain anymore
(Chin) And I don't want to participate
(Collarbone) But I don't want to be rude
(Under arm) And I don't know how to not participate

(Top of head) All this complaining
(Inner eyebrow) It's not solving anything
(Outer eye) It just makes me feel anxious
(Under eye) I'd like to stop complaining

(Under nose) But I don't know how

(Chin) I give myself permission

(Collarbone) To do what's best for me

(Under arm) To honor myself

Take a deep, cleansing breath. Recall again the complaining event. Notice how you feel now. Notice where in your body you feel it. Re-rate the intensity of the feelings, using the 1-10 scale. Notice any other thoughts or ideas that may have come up for you. Complaining may be deeply embedded in your mind and body. Complaining may be an old, old habit for you. Perhaps complaining is what your family does, and that's how you learned to fit in. It may take awhile, and lots of tapping to clear it out. Be kind and gentle with yourself and others as you learn to identify complaining and stop participating.

If the complaining continues, you can begin to say things to the complainer like, "Wow, I hear you. What are you going to do about it?" Or "I'm listening. What action are you going to take to change the situation?" These types of non-defensive statements really take the wind out of complaining. They may also alienate you from this person. As we change, others may not like it. We need to get comfortable in being our authentic selves.

We blame others.

When we blame others, we are judging them as being at fault, and we victimize ourselves. Blaming others implies that we had no part in the situation and no power. We always have a part in any situation in which we participate. Begin to take full responsibility for your part in things, and drop the blame.

If you truly had no part in the situation, perhaps you don't need to be involved at all.

We blame ourselves.

When we blame ourselves, we are judging ourselves as being at fault, and no one else has any responsibility, and that's how we make ourselves a victim. Blaming yourself is not the same as taking responsibility for your actions. Blaming yourself is usually an old habit that you learned - maybe when someone needed you to feel bad. They blamed you and you accepted the blame, rather than the responsibility. Can you feel the difference? Blame is powerless, responsibility is empowering. When we blame ourselves, we might say things like "This is just the way I am," or "Everyone in my family is like this," (which is both blaming ourselves and blaming our family) or "You couldn't possibly understand."

Exercise for when you've been blaming others.

When you've been blaming others, you've been giving your personal power away. Think of a time you blamed someone for something. It might have been a person you blamed, or an organization, or a company. This is NOT to suggest that they shouldn't take responsibility, or that what they did is ok. But you can let go of blaming them, take responsibility for your part in the situation, take back your personal power, and allow them to take back their personal power. Are you still holding onto that blame?

Try this tapping about that very blame situation. Use Ho'oponopono Hawaiian forgiveness technique combined with Tapping. They work great together.

Start tapping on the top of your head for this one:

(Top of head): I'm so sorry [insert your own name]

(Inner eyebrow): I apologize, [insert your own first name] for blaming you

(Outer eye): Please forgive me, [insert your own first name]

(Under eye): Thank you for forgiving me, [insert your own first name]

(Under nose): I love you, [insert your own first name]

(Chin): I want the very best for you, [insert your own first name]

Notice other ways that you judge others. If you are insisting on "being right," then you are judging the other person as "wrong." Do you try to "fix" others - letting them know that you know a better way? Do you ever say things like, "I would never do that!" or "I'm not that bad?" or "Why did you do that?" Becoming aware of judging is halfway to healing. Remember, you don't need to be perfect! Simply making progress in this area will have a profound effect on yourself, your circle of relationships, Humanity and the world!

#3 CLEAR YOUR CLUTTER

Definition of Clutter: *transitive verb: to fill or cover with scattered or disordered things that impede movement or reduce effectiveness*

~From Merriam Webster's online dictionary.

You might be wondering what clutter has to do with anything relating to changing the world. Clutter is a distraction from doing what you came here in this life to do - your Life Purpose. Clutter uses up a ton of mental energy and attention. Clutter wastes your time. Clutter is usually a hiding place for emotions, desires, and dreams, not to mention your car keys, that overdue electric bill, or the measuring tape.

If you have clutter like I did for much of my life, perhaps you think it's because you're a slob or a messy person. Maybe you think you're just not organized. Maybe you believe you can't get rid of anything. Maybe you're afraid of being neat as a pin like someone you grew up with (which you don't have to be when you clear your clutter). What if your clutter is a form of rebellion that you never grew out of? What if your clutter is a way for you to carve out some space for yourself? Whatever the root cause of your clutter, if it is keeping you from feeling free, from being truly creative, it is a problem. And if you're not feeling free, if you're not creating, you are in bondage to your stuff. From that place, you will likely feel like the world is unfair, or that you always have to work hard, or you can never catch up, or there's just no chance for you to get clarity, or to have a relationship - because of the mess.

Imagine what your life would be like if it were clutter-free or even mostly clutter-free. How much time would you save when you no longer have to look for things that are "lost" in your clutter? How often could you avoid having to "re-buy" something that you know you have but just can't find? How much less stress would you feel if you were more organized and could find things? How much more mind power would you have, once some of those projects and piles are finished or gone? What if you were surrounded only with things that you really love or that you really use?

CLUTTER COMES IN MANY FORMS

Clutter is a problem in most Western homes, offices, and cars. Garages and storage units are filled with forgotten items. Why do we have so much stuff? We thought it would bring us happiness, that's why. We bought into the propaganda they fed us. But all this stuff mostly causes us shame, frustrations, confusion, relationship problems, and it wastes our precious time and money. Most of us can't take care of all the stuff we have. Most of us can't even find a place to put all the stuff we have.

We buy bigger homes so we have more room for our stuff, and then we wonder why we're still not happy. We buy lots of stuff for our kids, and instead of spending quality time with them, we're either picking up their stuff, or nagging at them to do it.

Less stuff = more happiness!

How does stuff correlate with happiness? In 2017, the World Happiness Report http://worldhappiness.report/ed/2017/, compiled by the Organisation for Economic Co-operation and Development (OECD), showed that the US has dropped in rankings once again. In 2007 the US was ranked #3 in Happiness, but those rankings are currently at #14. The Happiness factors are: caring, freedom, generosity, honesty, health, income, and good governance.

China, despite increased average income, has not improved it's Happiness score in 25 years, so it's not simply a matter of making more money.

The desire for more stuff can certainly detract from caring and generosity amongst citizens and neighbors. And greed is a major factor in declining social support and increased corruption - two factors cited for the decline in US rankings for happiness. What about you? Do you find that having the stuff you think you want really makes you happy?

It is a widely recognized statistic that income up to $75,000 per year can proportionately increase happiness as it increases. But income above $75,000 per year does not generally increase happiness. Those income numbers and happiness aren't because of increased stuff, per se. Family, food, love, a home, education, access to nature, health care, elder care, care for disabled citizens, acceptance of other cultures, races, ethnicities, and religions - these are the things that really create happiness. After that, it's mostly just stuff!

Take a look around your living space, your office, your car - do you have lots of stuff? Is it stuff you really love? Or does your stuff work against your well-being? Consider clearing your clutter for greater happiness and enjoyment of life. If you are a happier, healthier being, you will have a greater, more positive impact on the people around you. And that will have a ripple effect.

Here are some tips and exercises to help you get started clearing your clutter. It's important to remember that clearing clutter is an ongoing proposition. Learning how to keep your spaces uncluttered takes practice and discipline. It's ok to ask for help with clearing clutter, cleaning your spaces, and learning how to be more organized.

#1 Clear small clutter areas at a time.
Small is relative. For some, a small area might be "just the dining room," while for others, small might be the top drawer in the kitchen - next to the sink.

#2 Use Tapping to help you alleviate overwhelm.
For many people, just looking at all the clutter can cause overwhelm. "Where do I begin?" "How do I begin?" "What will I do with the stuff I'm ready to get rid of?" "Who will I be without all my stuff?" These are they types of questions that can stop you in your tracks and keep you from clearing your clutter.

Here is a simple Tapping protocol for overwhelm due to clutter.
Reflect on your overall clutter. Without moving from where you're sitting, think of all the places you have clut-

ter. Know that noticing your feelings about your clutter is the first step in clearing it! Do you feel overwhelmed? Notice where in your body you feel that overwhelm feeling. Is it in your chest? Your head? Your stomach? There is no right or wrong place to feel. Just notice. And write down the feeling and where you feel it. Rate the intensity of your overwhelm using the 0-10 scale, with 0 being no intensity, and 10 being thoroughly overwhelmed, and write that number next to the emotion.

Tapping on the side of your hand, say these phrases:

Even though I have this clutter. All this clutter, I deeply and completely love and accept myself
Even though it feels overwhelming, I deeply and completely love and accept myself
Even though I don't know where to begin to clear this clutter, I love and accept myself, and I CHOOSE to feel peaceful, even if it's just while I'm doing this tapping. A little peace. A lot of peace. It all begins with me.

Now Tapping through the points, say one phrase at each point:

(Top of head) This clutter
(Inner eyebrow) This overwhelming clutter
(Outer eye) I don't know where or how to begin clearing this clutter
(Under eye) I've had this clutter for so long!
(Under nose) I wonder if it's keeping me protected from something -
(Chin) Maybe from looking at something
(Collarbone) Or from seeing something

(Under arm) Or from being seen

(Top of head) Or from finding something

(Inner eyebrow) I wonder if I'm hiding behind this clutter?

(Outer eye) Or maybe I'm rebelling in some way

(Under eye) Perhaps against someone who said it's not ok to be messy

(Under nose) Or maybe I'm fulfilling my belief that "I'm such a slob."

(Chin) Oh god, what a tangled mess!

(Collarbone) I wonder if it's possible to begin to untangle this mess, one strand at a time

(Under arm) With love and patience

(Top of head) Without the need to be perfect

Take a deep breath. Drink some water. Check back in with the feeling you wrote down. Do you still feel overwhelmed (or whatever your feeling was)? It's okay if you do, it's okay if you don't. Just notice again.

If you still feel that feeling, is it in the same place (head, chest, stomach, or wherever)? Re-rate the intensity of whatever the feeling is or was. Write down the new number. There are no right or wrongs in this protocol. You are entitled to whatever the intensity of feelings and emotions your are having. Jot down new number, and notes about anything else that came up for you during the round.

Repeat this Tapping round again, re-rating the intensity each time. If the intensity doesn't move, or moves very slowly, you probably need to shift your Tapping intention. If you tap this round three times, and don't get a shift in emotions, perspective or intensity, simply start again. Use the script above to help you, but insert words that mean more to you. Maybe you feel angry or powerless about the clutter in your life. Use one of those words and notice again where you feel it. Rate the intensity. Do the Tapping and re-rate the intensity.

You can use this script to tap on other stuff that came up – simply set that intention, and use these same words, or put in new words, or "rant and tap." Please don't rant and tap in front of anyone who might feel hurt by your words. I always recommend going into the bathroom, outside, or in the car to tap when others are around.

#3 Don't clear other people's clutter!

Especially not your kids. They need to participate in clutter clearing, or else they may feel betrayed. If you live with someone who collects clutter, but you feel that you don't collect clutter, please don't talk to your partner while you're angry or frustrated. And look at your own clutter first. Here's the thing: Usually super neat people make it clear from the get-go that they like things super neat. If you didn't do that, there's a good chance you aren't as super neat as you may think you are.

Either that, or you weren't able to express your needs at the outset of the relationship. If that is the case, this is another issue altogether, but it is your issue, not your partner's. For best results, do your own work first, then talk to your partner. For example, did you figure out why you couldn't speak your needs back then? Have you healed or resolved the root cause? If so, it's time to have a collaborative conversation with your partner, expressing what you used to be like, what happened, and what you're like now. And asking them if they can cooperate with meeting your needs. But these conversations should never be about blaming!

#4 Know that clutter-clearing, should you choose to accept it, will be a new lifestyle choice.

Once you get into the habit of living clutter free, it will be easier to keep up with. I have spent many years clearing clutter, downsizing, creating programs for helping people with their clutter, and being hired to actually help people with their clutter, yet I still have not resolved every clutter issue I have. But I have gotten to the root cause of much of my own clutter, and resolved those root issues, using Tapping. And I continue to practice!

You're not the boss of me!

I still find myself getting behind on paperwork. This is due to a very old, old issue of me wanting to do the fun stuff first. I describe it as "You're not the boss of me/I'm not the boss of me," and it originated when I was very young. I had no authority as a child - over myself or anything else. I was never asked my opinion or asked what I wanted or needed. Really not that unusual for the era in which I grew up. Almost everyone in our house was older than me, and so I got bossed around a lot. I'm sure I hated it and felt angry and frustrated about it. But I wasn't free to show my emotions or to speak them. Again, not that unusual at that time. Although I don't remember ever saying it, I see myself at 4 or 5 years old, standing with my hands on my hips saying "You're not the boss of me!"

So imagine my little kid self growing up, never wanting anyone to tell me what to do. And unconsciously I took this way too far. I couldn't even tell *myself* what to do! That little girl with her hands on her hips was offering "You're not the boss of me!" to even her adult self. And oddly, her adult self (me) went along with it.

That may sound ridiculous, but I know so many people who suffer from "You're not the boss of me/I'm not the boss of me" in many areas of their lives, including clutter, food, money, and more. We just weren't given any authority or taught self-mastery as children. But it's never too late to heal and to learn. Self-mastery is another topic for another book. But with regard to clutter, you will likely need to overcome some old mental habits in order to clear your clutter. And Tapping is great for doing just that.

#5 You don't need to be "neat as a pin."

The idea is to cull your stuff, lighten your load, eliminate your distractions. You don't need to do it perfectly. There are very few people who are neat-as-a-pin naturally. And unless that's something you aspire to, I encourage you to set a more reasonable goal.

You may want to set a limit for the things you have lots of. 10 shirts, 10 pairs of shoes, 5 purses, only keep the makeup I actually use, all car and house keys organized and located in the same place, 3 sets of towels, 2 sets of sheets for each bed. Or whatever is both reasonable for you and still allows you to get rid of some of your unnecesary stuff. Again, don't try to do it all at once!

I once knew a woman who, when you went into her house, it appeared she was super neat and organized. As I got to know her better, she admitted to me her housekeeping strategies. For one thing, when she wanted to clean in a hurry, or was helping someone else clean up their mess, she would put all loose items into smaller tubs or containers, put a lid on the containers, and place them into a closet or cupboard. Stuffing our stuff behind closed doors is like stuffing our emotions. Think of your style of clutter and housekeeping as a metaphor for your emotional well-being. My style of clutter, like my emotional well-being, was an eclectic jumble of wanted and unwanted stuff, usually on display in ways that lowered my self-esteem and embarrassed me. What are you hiding? What does your clutter keep you distracted from?

As you address your clutter, be kind and gentle with yourself, and yet be firm. If you let yourself always "get away" with not clearing your clutter or neatening your mess, it's like letting a child always have cookies for breakfast. It doesn't set good boundaries, and it's not very healthy. Children feel secure with healthy boundaries that allow them to safely make some decisions for themselves, and to learn from their mistakes. If you weren't given those kinds of boundaries as a child, most likely there are symptoms of it in your adult life.

Forgive the past and lovingly begin setting boundaries for yourself now. Make a decision to begin to clear your clutter now, and see what happens in your inner world. And your outer world!

For more information, check out my "Clear Your Clutter with Tapping" 15-part audio/video program here: HelenMcConnell.com/programs

CHAPTER FOUR

FOCUS ON WHAT YOU'RE *FOR* (LAW OF ATTRACTION)

"All that we are is a result of what we have thought."

~ Gautama Buddha

An EEG (electroencephalogram) is a machine that detects electrical activity in your brain using small, flat metal discs (electrodes) attached to your scalp. Your brain cells communicate via electrical impulses and are active all the time, even when you're asleep. This activity is known as thought. Thought activity shows up as wavy lines on an EEG recording. Thoughts create energy - that's how they show up on the recording!

Your heart also creates electrical impulses, in the same manner, (energy) which are measured by an EKG or ECG (electrocardiogram). The signal to create electrical impulses comes from the brain and through the nervous systems (both sympathetic and parasympathetic) which "tell" the heart to speed up or slow down, depending on physical activity, stress, and rest. These are the signals that show up on the EKG. So you can see that emotions create energy! As if we didn't know that already!

That energy from your thoughts and emotions is what creates your reality. Your reality is different than anyone else's reality, although you may think they are the same or similar. Each person sees their reality through their own set of mental and emotional filters. These filters are created through life experiences, family beliefs, cultural beliefs, and through our own personality. The combinations of these experiences are infinite! And therefore, there are infinite realities.

We humans have anywhere from 50,000 - 70,000 or more thoughts every day. I suppose you could argue the numbers - how are thoughts counted? What constitutes a thought? When does one thought begin and one end? etc. The research consistently reports these numbers - 50,000 to 70,000 thoughts a day, or more. But no matter how you count thoughts, the fact is, we know we are thinking all the time. This includes our conscious and subconscious thoughts, and it has been determined that we mostly think "subconscious" thoughts. And for most of us, most of those subconscious thoughts are negative and repetitive. Most people have a powerful subconscious "programming" that is negative, repetitive, compulsive. So what kind of reality do you think comes from that type of powerful thinking? Yep, a negative, repetitive, compulsive reality.

We are sending out energetic signals all the time, drawing what is energetically similar back to us. This is the essence of the Law of Attraction, or Law of Magnetism. We are like radio broadcasting towers - sending out the signals for our unique radio station. And if we want to receive the likes of station 101.7, we need to send out similar frequencies. Any other setting will create static, or bring in another station all together.

If you're too young to remember radio dials, use a 21st Century metaphor: If you want Google to search for the ten best restaurants in your area, you've got to put in the correct search criteria. Or at least be close, like "Top local eateries," or "great places to eat.". If you ask Google to "find auto repair shops," you're not going to get the results you wanted, no matter how many times you search. You're asking Google to focus on "car repair," but wanting Google to give you "great places to eat."

WHAT ARE YOU BROADCASTING?

If you want to attract something into your life, I encourage you to focus on what you're FOR, rather than what you're against. Most people talk about what they're "for" in terms of what they're against. They say things like, "All the good partners are taken," and "I'm against the war," and "I wish I could buy that car, but it's too expensive," and "I wish I weren't in pain!" and "I don't want to get cancer like everyone else in my family." Those phrases are focusing on what we don't want - 'no good partners', 'war', 'cars that are too expensive', 'pain,' 'cancer'.

Despite the fact that they might think they are asking for what they want, they are still sending out energetic frequencies of "no good partners," "the war," and cars that I can't afford." Even if we change the wording to "I wish I could find a good partner," we're still sending out the frequency of "no good partner." "I wish I could afford that car," still has the energy of "I can't afford that car." The sentiment, or energy of these messages is still "lack." And lack is what we will continue to attract.

If you're sending out "I can't afford that car," there is also a lot of negative emotion attached to it. And that emotion intensifies the frequency. And this is true whether you're saying it out loud, or simply thinking it. Or even if you avoid thinking about what you want - that also sends out a frequency of "I can't have it."

Try saying "I choose vibrant health." "I love being vibrantly healthy." "I love my body".

The same is true if you're feeling frightened about situations that are going on around the globe. You (and a lot of other people as well) are sending negative energy to that thing you don't like. If there is a world leader who you don't like, I suggest you talk about her from a perspective of what you're for, rather than what you're against. For example, say "I am for basic rights for all human beings," rather than "I'm joining an anti-human-rights rally." I agree that sometimes "anti" rallies get results. But that's due, in great part, because we're so programmed to think that way, and our world leaders won't give in unless there's violence. It doesn't have to be that way. Give attention to what you're for. If you're not the kind of person to attend such a rally, don't watch it on the internet. Send your loving thoughts and healing prayers to what you're for. And even if you aren't for something you hear about, send loving thoughts to it anyway. Your choice is to send love, or send fear - those are really the only two emotions. You will either be adding fear to the energy, or love. Love really does heal all.

When we think about what we're against, even if we're saying we don't want it, we are still sending out the energetic signal of that very thing we're against, because we can't think about "I wish I could afford it" without thinking about "not having enough money." So begin now to learn to think of what you're really for. For example, "I love feeling healthy!," "I LOVE that car!." "I love the feeling of being in an intimate, loving relationship," "I love having plenty of money to be able to travel," etc. But we can think about "I love driving that car!" or "I can see myself walking hand-in-hand with my partner," and that's a totally different frequency.

I'm NOT suggesting that you go out and buy a car (or anything else) that you don't currently have the money for. But move your thinking and your feeling toward what you want, and focus on that feeling for as long as possible. 68 seconds of concentrated focus of thought and feeling will bring your manifestation closer to you. Feeling about what you want as if you already have it is the most powerful tool you have.

This idea of focusing on what you're for is the best way to attract what you want into your life. If you want more money, focus on being wealthy, not on how poor you are. If you've got a cold, focus on being well, not how bad you feel. If you hate being stuck in traffic, focus on "smooth sailing," not how frustrated you feel.

Focusing on what you're for is all well and good when you're conscious of what you're thinking and saying. But what about all the other times - when you're thinking unconsciously? As I said earlier, we have mostly unconscious thoughts. And most are negative and repetitive. So we are mostly attracting things into our lives that we don't want.

What are we to do about all those unconscious thoughts? If we're not really aware of them, how are we to change them? If you want to know what you're thinking about, notice how you feel and what's showing up for you. If you're feeling uncomfortable or having negative feelings, then you're thinking about things that are uncomfortable, or you're thinking negative thoughts - whether or not you realize it. It's really that simple! Look at your life. Do you attract what you want? Do you live joyously? Do you have vibrant health? If not, then your primary vibration is less than what you really want. Everything we attract into our lives is a reflection of our energy.

I'm not suggesting that if you've had a car accident this week that you wanted to have a car accident. But it's important to know that you attracted it into your life, along with anyone else who was involved. And they attracted it into their life too. Not consciously, of course! Your conscious thoughts are not your most powerful ones. And you probably didn't "want" an accident even at the unconscious level. But whatever you've been thinking about and feeling, has mostly been at the frequency of the accident. The Universe has a much bigger viewpoint than we do. Maybe you wanted to get out of doing something, but you're not comfortable saying "no." Seriously, if that is a big problem for you, your subconscious mind will devise ways for you to get out of it, even if it means having an accident.

A few months ago, I met with a friend for lunch. She asked me how I was doing. I'd been having a lot of "bad hair days" in a row, my clothes didn't fit right, and my makeup felt rushed. So I said "I feel like a wreck!" Two days later, while riding my bike, I was hit by a car. Was I asking to be hit by a car? Not exactly, no. But I was exuding the feeling of "being a wreck" and my reality continued to match that frequency.

Now I say "I feel like a million bucks!" no matter what's going on in my life!

From that accident and the injuries I sustained, I had to slow down, rest, and ask for help - things that don't come easily to me because of underlying beliefs. I guess the Universe had to get my attention somehow! And yes, I've been using Tapping on those.

We don't manifest instantly, and that's a good thing. Otherwise, when we we're driving on the freeway, we would be causing horrible accidents all around us as we wish that guy would die, or prophesize that "they are going to kill someone." And we don't always manifest exactly the way we think we want something to arrive. There is a time-delay between desiring something and manifesting it materially. And the Universe has way bigger plans than we do.

But the Law of Attraction is always working - it's just like the law of Gravity. Think about Gravity. It works whether we're a good person or a bad person. It works whether we're paying attention to it or not. Gravity requires no effort on our part. And when we work with Gravity for things like flying an airplane, magnificent things happen. The Law of Attraction works whether we're a good person or a bad person. It works whether we're paying attention to it or not. It requires no effort on our part. And when we work with the Law of Attraction (what we're for), magnificent things and situations manifest!

The Law of Attraction isn't just about getting what you say you want. The Law of Attraction is always drawing to us that which aligns with our dominant vibrational frequency. And often, that frequency is more about what we don't want. So begin to learn to focus on what you want.

Take a look at what's showing up in your life. Notice how it feels to think about these things that are showing up. And know that your dominant vibration is matching what's showing up. Also know that other people are manifesting in their lives, and they may need you to be a willing or unwilling participant in order to manifest. For example, recently my dear friend's lovely American Staffordshire Terrier died very suddenly. My friend was shocked and heartbroken. Did she manifest shock and heartbreak? Not consciously, no. But she has been asking for some really big dreams to start manifesting, and the Universe knows what she needs to move forward. The shock and heartbreak may be just the thing she needed to get out of her comfort zone. I don't profess to know all the things the Universe unfolds for us. It was her dog's time to die. My friend didn't manifest that. And yet, when she got her lovely pooch, my friend was aware that at some time in the future, the dog would die. And it would likely be before she herself died. What has come from this seemingly sad event is that my friend's dad was in his final weeks when my friend's dog died. The death of the dog brought her dad to a new understanding of the Divine. He was able to be there for my friend in her time of need, even though he was experiencing his final days. For that, my friend is extremely grateful. And if you had known her dog, you would just know that he was a lovingly willing participant in the unfolding.

If you've got old unconscious thought patterns running (and you do), you may not even realize it. Each of us has a sort of protection mechanism within us that keeps us from seeing our unconscious patterns. Because, you see, the subconscious mind senses change as dangerous. So it creates all sorts of things to keep us from changing - even if it means making us defy our dreams.

The conflict is that we love for things to change, we love variety, we love innovation. So how do we resolve this inner conflict? How do we get our powerful subconscious mind to go along with our conscious mind? How do we stop the self-sabotage? How do we get our mind to begin to focus on what we're for? I use Tapping, and you can too.

Let's do some Tapping for the inner conflict between what we say we want, and our subconscious programming which may "believe" differently.

First, let's do some Tapping to help loosen up our attachment to focusing on what we're against. This is a strong cultural, societal, and often familial "habit." If you heard your father and your grandmother always talking about the negative stuff, that kind of talk feels familiar (in the truest sense of the word) and "normal" to you. But I promise you, it's not helping you, or the world. You might argue that it's just the way things are. But that's only your perspective. And maybe you don't have to be so focused on reality all the time! It's often helpful to feel into a more glorious future. Now seemingly in contradiction to that, we'll tap the negative first. With Tapping, we get to the negative and address it. If you aren't feeling negative at any level, it won't hurt you to do this Tapping. If you have a partial or full reaction to the negative, we're on the right track!

Let's Tap.

Tapping on the side of the hand, say each of these phrases:

Even though I habitually think and say negative things, I accept myself completely
Even though that's a deeply-rooted habit, I love and accept myself
Even though I'm not even aware of how often I go negative, I love and accept myself

Now, Tapping around the points, say one phrase at each point:

(Top of head) These negative thoughts and words
(Inner eyebrow) My glass is half-empty
(Outer eye) I need to watch out for all the negative things in the world
(Under eye) I need to protect myself
(Under nose) I need to be hyper-vigilant
(Chin) I don't know who I'd be if I didn't think such negative thoughts
(Collarbone) Thinking and saying negative things is a habit
(Under arm) I need to be unhappy now - just in case something happens

(Top of head) My parents were negative
(Inner eyebrow) I learned it from them
(Outer eye) They wouldn't like it if I stopped being negative
(Under eye) They'd think I was weird
(Under nose) My friends are all negative
(Chin) How will I have a conversation?
(Collarbone) I don't really want to give up being negative
(Under arm) I like looking out for the worst

Take a deep breath. This protocol is meant to be really negative - to express possible thoughts you might have about focusing on what you're for. By tapping the negative, you will become more aware of it, and you'll be able to make a choice about how you want to be, rather than simply responding from habit. And again, if you don't have any of this negativity at any level, it won't make you negative when you do this Tapping.

Let's do a protocol to acknowledge the inner conflict about "I want things to change," "I don't like change." There is one thing that is consistently true - everything changes. I call this protocol "back and forth tapping." You'll see why. It's meant to shake up your thinking a bit, and actually help you sense more clearly what you want.

For this protocol, we'll begin on the top of the head, tapping one point for each phrase below:

(Top of head): I want things to change
(Inner eyebrow): I don't want anything to change
(Outer eye): I like change
(Under eye): I don't like change
(Under nose): I embrace change
(Chin): I resist change
(Collarbone): Change is good
(Under arm): Change is frightening

(Top of head): I don't want change
(Inner eyebrow): I love change
(Outer eye): I want everything to stay the same
(Under eye): Change is exciting
(Under nose): I resist change
(Chin): I like change
(Collarbone): Change is scary

phrases as you tap. Do two rounds. Start with positive on the first round, and start with negative on the second round. That way, you will have tapped a positive and a negative phrase at each of the Tapping points.

When we want to change anything in our lives, we have to change our *thinking*. *This is the single most-important idea in this whole book!* Read it over again until you understand it. When we want to change anything in our lives, we have to change our *thinking*.

This is true for the smallest change - like making a right turn at the corner instead of turning left - or for bigger changes - like losing weight or learning to be successful. But how do we change our thinking? Most of us change our thinking at a snail's pace, and that just isn't fast enough to make the changes we want in our lives! And so we get discouraged and give up even trying to change. So I created this "Thought Interruption Protocol (TIP) Tapping, to make the process faster.

Tapping for changing your thinking.

Focus on something in your life you want to change - something you have responsibility for - like a habit or your money situation. Notice that it's your old habitual thinking that has got you stuck. It is just your thinking, nothing else. Notice how that old thinking feels. In other words, when you are stuck in habitual thinking or action, what does it feel like in your head or in your body. I get a sensation in my head that feels likes a tug to the left. Everyone has their own way of recognizing it. Notice your own sensations. Now tap on that old habitual thinking:

(Top of head): *There's* some old thinking!

(Inner eyebrow): Habitual, repetitive unconscious thinking

(Outer eye): I've been thinking this same way for a long time

(Under eye): And wondering why things aren't changing

(Under nose): I'm ready to let this old thinking go

(Chin): I'm choosing to let this old thinking go

(Collarbone): I'm choosing new thinking

(Under arm): And I don't need to figure out what that new thinking is

(Top of head): I can't figure out the new thinking

(Inner eyebrow): Because I only know how to think in this same old way

(Outer eye): But I'm choosing to open to infinite thinking

(Under eye): To Divine thinking

(Under nose): I'm opening my mind to the Source of all thinking

(Chin): The Source of all ideas

(Collarbone): I'm choosing new thinking

(Under arm): And I don't need to figure out what that new thinking is

Take a deep breath. This Tapping protocol can be shortened to 4 phrases, tapping while you say them:

(Top of head) There's some old thinking

(Inner eyebrow) I'm ready to let this old thinking go

(Outer eye) I'm choosing to let it go

(Under eye) I'm choosing Divine thinking now!

Use this protocol often! Like several times a day. It's great not only for changing your negative thinking, but your limited thinking too. It can reduce or eliminate cravings, get you started on your exercise plan, and get you back to work when you've been distracted. "A change in perspective is where miracles happen."

Start your day by identifying what you're for today!

#5 HAVE FUN!

*People rarely succeed unless they have fun
in what they are doing."*

~Dale Carnegie

That's right, if you want to profoundly change the world, have
more fun. The kind of fun that makes you belly-laugh. Or the
kind of fun that brings you deep joy. Whatever fun means to
you, because it's not the same for everyone, have more of it.

"Why would this possibly change the world?" you ask.

Throughout this book you are learning steps that change
the world "out there" by changing the world "in here." When
our inside world changes, our outside world changes. If you
want a happier world "out there," you've got to create a happier world "in here."

As the wisdom of the ancients said, "As above, so below.
As within, so without."

I can hear some of you saying, "But I can't be having more
fun when the world is in the shape it's in. I can't be happy
when people are starving! I can't feel good when people are
suffering."

I hear this argument all the time. I used to believe in this argument. But I've discovered that this belief - that I can't be happy while people are suffering - is wrong. This really is the main point of this book - to help you to realize that your outer world is a reflection of your inner world.

Think of it this way: You can't be miserable enough to help make miserable people happy. You can't feel bad enough to help make your sad friends feel better. You can't be broke enough to help make poor people rich. You can't be sick enough to help your sick friends feel better. You've got to make yourself happy first!

Have fun! It all begins with YOU!

Imagine a large lake. You are in the center of the vast expanse of water. From you, every time you touch the lake, it creates ripples outward. Your life, your reality is like the lake. Everything you think or feel or say or do ripples out around you. You may not realize what happens to the ripples - they leave your field of vision and hearing and sensing - but they are still rippling. What you think about today creates your reality tomorrow or the next day or the next year.

As the ripples get to the shore, they begin rippling back toward the center of the lake. What you think about and feel about goes out and out and out, and then comes back to you. Not as an exact duplicate of your thoughts and emotions, but as a vibrational match to the vibration of your thoughts and emotions. And as you focus on your thoughts and emotions, they get magnified. And the returning ripples also get magnified. So, if you are focused on how angry you still are at your parents for something they did when you were 6 or 16 or 26, become aware of the ripple effect of that anger in your own life. That's your creation! Your parents may have provided you with the opportunity to be angry, but it is you who have fueled your emotions all this time. Fuel you could be using to create something much more wonderful.

Now that you're aware of how you create your reality, isn't it time to start deliberately creating yours, rather than defaulting to old thoughts and emotions?

So why have fun? Why not get serious about creating your reality? Weren't you taught that you have to work hard before you can have fun? Well, you certainly can get serious about creating your reality, and you will attract more to feel serious about. If you make a decision to have more fun no matter what, you will attract more fun into your life.

FIND YOUR OWN KIND OF FUN!

Fun doesn't look the same for all people. Not everyone enjoys going dancing or doing karaoke. Some people enjoy a quiet evening at home with friends, playing Scrabble. Some enjoy a sporting event. Some people find their fun on the ski slopes, or on a bike. Some enjoy reading a good book, or watching a movie, making love, petting the cat, painting. Whatever brings you enjoyment - do more of that.

For many years of my life, I used to say that it was fun for me to go to a bar and get drunk. I did a lot of that. But even though I laughed a lot in those days, I wasn't really having fun. I was numbing my feelings. I did not feel comfortable in my own skin until I was liquored up or stoned. In the short run, I had some fun. In the medium run (looking back the following day), I usually felt remorse and shame. In the long run, that 17-year period of my life when I drank alcoholically, seems such a waste (pun intended!).

Also during those years, I often had fun at the expense of other people - ridiculing, judging, looking down my drunken nose, gossiping. Again, this is soul-sucking kind of fun. Not what I'm recommending here.

So if you've been having fun at the expense of others, I urge you to reclaim your humor. If you've been overindulging in alcohol or drugs in order to "have fun," I invite you to get really honest with yourself and do something different. Don't kid yourself...bingeing on anything isn't fun.

Have real fun. Discover or rediscover your joy. Find someone to enjoy yourself with. Learn something new. Take a class. Go salsa dancing. Join a singing Meetup. Get your health back. Go for a walk. Work in your garden. Ride your bike. Attend a concert. Explore a book store or museum. On a rainy day. (and we have lots of them here in Portland) I like to put on my rain boots and go puddle-stomping, or ride my bike. Most people don't take the time to have that kind of silly fun.

Perhaps you've been giving too much attention to things that make you unhappy? In Chapter 4, you learned to turn away from what you're against and turn toward what you're for. This is the time to suggest that you stop watching the news on TV or internet. Amongst my clients and workshop participants, the news is one of the greatest sources of anxiety, stress, and unhappiness. And like a wreck on the side of the freeway, it's almost impossible to turn away from the news, even if it makes you feel bad. But it's not impossible to stop watching the news, I promise you. If you feel that it's just too much to give up the news permanently, try it on a temporary basis. Try this experiment:

7-Day News Detox.
- Make a decision to give yourself a 7-day break from the news
- Include tv, internet, radio, and newspaper
- Notice your nervous system over the course of the week. Do you feel less stressed? Less fearful? Less gloomy?
- Notice that you still hear about news events, even if you don't look for them on media.
- Notice if you "miss" hearing the news

At the end of your 7-day news detox, consider repeating it, or try the:

7-Day Media Detox.

This follows the same guidelines as the 7-Day News Detox, but you also include a break from all social media.

After your detox, like a food detox, begin adding in one medium at a time. Or start by limiting your exposure to a certain number of minutes per day. Each of these experiments will give you clear insight to your reliance upon/addiction to media.

Notice what you replace your media time with. The first time I did a media detox, I found myself watching Netflix incessantly. When I decided to detox from Netflix, I filled in with YouTube videos. I now consider Netflix and YouTube social media. When I finally got free of them all, I found that I also stopped bingeing on cookies and other food. I can now watch occasional YouTube, but I have to really monitor myself. And I limit my Netflix viewing.

Consider using your "free" time to go for a short walk several times a day. Or do short (3-4 minute) meditations throughout your day. Practice deep breathing. Clean your cupboards. Take a nap. Have more sex. Get your creative on. Read a book. And definitely use your time to do more fun things! Give yourself permission to try one new fun thing each week.

YOU ARE EXISTING IN A TRANCE

What if I told you that you have been brainwashed and that, for the most part, someone else is doing all your thinking for you? It's true. Individually and collectively, we are in a trance most of the time. When you're in a trance, you may think you're doing your own thinking, but any thoughts you have are habitual, repetitive, and likely originated with someone else.

Advertisers figured out how to brainwash their audience a long time ago. Images, songs, emotional messages, catchy phrases, sexy people are just some of the ways they get us to want to buy their products.

Politics, patriotism, propaganda. Consider each "issue" you are passionate about. Do more research to find out the real facts. I promise you, if your primary and secondary education was in the U.S., you've not been given all the facts, but rather a skewed version that "they" (whoever "they" are) want you to learn. This is true in history, health, and even science. It's not easy to let loose of your long-held beliefs, but I encourage you to get less attached to them, to be open to a deeper truth.

Here are some of the ways you can tell that you or others are in a trance.

When you're talking with someone, and you can't really hear what the other person is saying, or they can't really hear what you are saying, one or both of your are in a trance. If you find yourself thinking about what you are going to say when there's a break in the conversation, you are not hearing what the other person is saying and meaning, and you are in a trance. This is also true if the person you are talking to talks back to you but doesn't respond to what you were saying, but rather just "says something."

Whenever you are watching media, you are in a trance. You cannot be aware of what you're feeling, or what it is going on around you if you are watching a movie or a YouTube video.

If you check out of your body for any reason, you are in a trance of sorts. Often this is your built-in protection mechanism against traumatic memories. Don't force a change here, but become aware. Seek help for traumatic memories. Tapping, in the hands of a skilled practitioner, is one of the most powerful tools for this.

When you get stuck in a rut of thoughts and feelings, you are caught up in unconscious thinking. You are in a trance.

Most people, when they are talking on their phones, are mostly in a trance. You may think you're a good driver when you're on the phone, but you're not!

If you find yourself "lost in thought," you are in a trance. This isn't always a negative, but become aware of where your thoughts are taking you. If you suddenly find yourself down the rabbit hole of negativity, the thoughts you are lost in aren't serving you. But if, on the other hand, you are experiencing inspirations and "aha! Moments" as you wander in your thoughts, these are more helpful to you.

Just about anytime you're staring at your screen, you are in a trance.

The common thread behind each of these 10 Simple Things is to help you become more conscious. More aware. More awakened and enlightened. To think new thoughts and have new conversations. To get to know other people and really hear what they're saying and meaning. Laughter and having fun is a great way to get free of your trance.

IT'S TIME TO AWAKEN!

Two blocks from where I live is a Whole Foods Market. If I'm hungry, or even if I just want something to eat (emotional eating), I can walk over and get some food. I sometimes find myself in the cookie aisle before I even realize I've left the house. Sometimes I've eaten half the bag of cookies (which are healthy, by the way, because they come from Whole Foods) while I'm still in a trance. I haven't consciously thought about the consequences of what I'm about to do, or what I'm doing. I haven't asked myself if this is what I really want to do, or is it just an old habit. I have walked to the store, bought cookies, and eaten half of them, all in an unconscious trance!

I used to think that if I just had enough willpower, I could stop myself. But willpower alone doesn't work. My old thinking is deeply habitual, unconscious, repetitive, and very, very negative. And I realized that if I want anything to change, I've got to change my thinking.

For years I wondered how to change my behavior. When willpower didn't work, I'd berate myself for being weak and broken. Sometimes I'd remember that I had been able to stop drinking alcohol and hadn't had a drink in over 30 years. But I'd think back and realize that I tried many times to stop - I tried willpower and I tried other tricks to get myself to not drink. None of them worked for more than a couple of days.

When I finally stopped drinking, it was because I'd had an epiphany - a moment of such clarity that it changed my life forever. My thinking was changed in a way that didn't require the use of willpower or force.

I'd given up cocaine cold turkey, out of deep fear. I got "scared straight" when I learned of a young college basketball player using cocaine one time and having a heart attack and dying. I wasn't nearly as healthy as that young man, so I just knew my time would be soon. I guess I wanted to live more than I wanted to do cocaine. My thinking was changed in an instant.

If I tried to quit smoking once, I tried a hundred times. But I kept trying. I tried nicotine patches and nicotine gum, hypnosis, not smoking in the car, only smoking in the car, not smoking when I drank, only smoking when I drank, and all sorts of other tricks to get myself to quit. The day I finally stopped for good, I knew I wouldn't smoke again. Something in me had transformed. My thinking about smoking, and about not smoking, had changed. Drastically. I've never had another cigarette since. Nor have I ever wanted one!

So why can't I do the same about cookies? Or about NetFlix? Or about any other "habit" that feels disempowering or downright unhealthy? It's because I haven't changed my deepest thinking about those things yet. I say "yet" because I intend to keep at it until I do.

Until recently, I didn't know how to change my thinking at all. I tried saying affirmations, listening to recordings, hypnosis. I just couldn't get myself to repeat things often enough and for long enough to get the message down into my subconscious mind, where the trance-like thinking originates.

Something down in that place tells me that eating cookies is a really good idea right now.

But I have discovered a way to temporarily interrupt my "cookie thinking." It does take some practice and some diligence. But it's such a short protocol, I have been able to use it for many things. And since it's such an important piece of self-change work, I've included this protocol in more than one chapter.

[Author's note: I'm delighted to report that I haven't had a cookie in over 3 months. And I haven't even missed them! In fact, I hadn't even thought about them until I was doing the final editing of this chapter! The Tapping below is very effective!]

Tapping for when you find yourself stuck in old, patterned thinking.

Here are some Tapping protocols to help you get out of your trance, and to lighten up and have more fun!

Begin by *noticing* how it feels when you have old thinking. You don't even need to be aware of *what* you're thinking about, just *that* you're thinking repetitive thoughts. I notice, for example, that I hum repetitively, no real tune, when I'm thinking old repetitive thoughts. Or I find myself in front of the refrigerator, just an hour after my last meal. I've also learned to recognize a particular feeling in my body - it's like my left ear is being gently pulled down to my left shoulder - when I'm thinking negative old thoughts. If you can't yet notice anything, that's okay. Know that there is a really good chance that you are, right now in this moment, thinking old, repetitive, negative thoughts, and that in any case, this tapping won't be bad for you.

Practice using this Tapping protocol until you can use it *before* you buy those cookies, and preferably before you even leave the house to go buy those cookies. But you can use it in the grocery store. Don't worry, no one is watching you. Use this whenever you find yourself unconsciously sitting in front of your computer screen, binge-watching Netflix. All it takes is enough willpower to get yourself to tap one round. One simple round, less than a minute. The more often you do this protocol, the easier it will become to break your trance.

Tapping around the points, beginning at the top of your head, say the following as you tap:

(Top of head): *There's* some old thinking
(Inner eyebrow): Old, repetitive thinking
(Outer eye): Negative, habitual thinking
(Under eye): I'm not even sure what I'm thinking about
(Under nose): But I know I've had these same thoughts many times
(Chin): Same old thoughts, over and over
(Collarbone): And then I wonder why I get the same results
(Under arm): This old thinking isn't serving me
(Top of head): I'm ready to let this old thinking go
(Inner eyebrow): I'm choosing to let it go now
(Outer eye): I'm choosing new thinking
(Under eye): And I don't need to figure out what that new thinking is
(Under nose): I'm open to Infinite Thinking
(Chin): Beyond anything I could figure out
(Collarbone): There's so much more for me
(Under arm): Beyond my own limited thinking

Take a deep breath. Notice any sensation from that Tapping. Many people report a sort of mental sigh of relief when they do this. Like their brain was just waiting for permission to take a little break. And most people find it an even greater relief to know that "I don't need to figure it out."

Here's some Tapping for people who think "I don't know how to have fun," or "I'm just not a fun person."

Sense into how true it feels when you think "I don't know how to have fun," or "I'm just not a fun person."

Tapping on the side of the hand point, say the following:

Even though I'm not a fun person, I love and accept my not-fun self

Even though I don't think I know how to have fun, I love and accept my not-fun self

Even though I'm not sure I can have fun, I love and accept my not-fun self

(Top of head): I don't know how to have fun

(Inner eyebrow): Everyone else knows how to have fun

(Outer eye): I'm just not a fun person

(Under eye): I've never had fun in my life!

(Under nose): I've never known how to have fun

(Chin): I'm just not a fun person

(Collarbone): I'll leave the fun for everyone else

(Under arm): I don't know how to have fun!

Take a deep breath in. Often by simply Tapping the "story" we tell about ourselves, our mind gives us reminders that the story is not completely true. Like, "I do *too* know how to have fun," and "I've had fun lots of times," and so on. Notice what came up for you as you tapped that round. Perhaps you got a memory of sometime in the past when you had lots of fun. See, you do know how to have fun! Just be yourself. Some people are more serious than others. That's a beautiful thing. We're not all meant to be the life of the party. Or to even enjoy going to the party.

Here's some Tapping for when you think you shouldn't have fun, because of all the things that are going on in the world.

Sense into any part of you that thinks you shouldn't have fun - for any reason. Now do this Tapping:

(Top of head): I should not be having fun
(Inner eyebrow): It's not appropriate for me to have fun
(Outer eye): People are suffering
(Under eye): People are grieving
(Under nose): I should be suffering with them
(Chin): I should be grieving with them
(Collarbone): I should not be having fun
(Under arm): It's not ok for me to have fun!

(Top of head): It's more helpful if I suffer
(Inner eyebrow): It's more helpful if I grieve
(Outer eye): If I suffer more, maybe they'll feel better
(Under eye): If I grieve more, maybe they'll feel better
(Under nose): Whatever I do, I should not have fun
(Chin): No fun for me!
(Collarbone): I'll leave the fun for everyone else
(Under arm): I shouldn't be having fun!

Take a deep breath. Okay, you probably sensed the sarcasm in that round. We use this type of approach in Tapping to help us discover our inner argument, and help us tease out how we really want to feel. Remember, focus on what you're for, not what you're against!

And finally, some Tapping to give yourself permission to have fun.

Do you need permission to have fun? Is there someone in your life who expects you to not have fun, or doesn't like it when you do? That is their old thinking, but it doesn't have to be yours.

Begin by tapping on the side of your hand:

Even though I've been taught that I shouldn't be having fun, I love and accept my fun self
Even though people have told me it's not ok to have fun, I love and accept my fun self
Even though I'm not sure I should have fun, I love and accept my fun self!

(Top of head): I want to have fun
(Inner eyebrow): Even if others are suffering
(Outer eye): I want to have some fun
(Under eye): In my own way
(Under nose): I give myself permission to have fun
(Chin): To create fun in the world
(Collarbone): Because fun can heal the suffering
(Under arm): Fun can heal the grieving

Take a deep breath and notice how each of these Tapping protocols made you feel. It really is ok to have fun - even if others are suffering. There are some amazing stories from concentration camps where prisoners had fun to keep their spirits up, and to cheer up those around them. And those people had a much higher survival rate.

And in your everyday life, having fun is so important. Even at work. *Especially* at work. Don't take life so seriously! Have more fun! As you go out today, see if there are ways you can have more fun and make other people smile!

#6 CULTIVATE A POSITIVE MIND

"What we think, we become."

~Gautama Buddha

You may have noticed that all 10 Simple Steps in this book have ultimately been about cultivating a positive mind. A positive mind is when we can view or experience a situation and, even if the situation is negative in nature, discover something positive in it. Maybe not right in the moment, but at some point we recognize that every moment offers something special. We may not like that thing, but we can acknowledge that it is a gift from some perspective. Sometimes it takes many years to recognize the gift in a crappy situation. Like when you got fired from that job and you didn't notice until two years later that being fired had opened you up to starting your own business that you now love. The gift may not always be that obvious, and it may take a shorter time or a longer time (or even another lifetime), but there is a gift in every moment, in every event.

It's not easy to cultivate this positive mind, in part because we're trained to look for the negative. But even if we're attempting to cultivate a positive mind, the world is quick to say things like "Do you always have to be so positive?" like it's a bad thing. Most people want to feel bad, even if they don't realize it, and they want to bring everyone around them down with them. You get to choose if you're going there or not.

Notice your languaging and your thoughts. Do your words and thoughts lean towards possibilities? Or do they lean more towards "I doubt it." For example, do you use phrases like "I can't," "It's so hard," "I don't like," "I never,"?

If you are a "glass half empty" kind of person, it may be a matter of old habitual thoughts and beliefs. You can notice and catch yourself and say "I'd like to," or "I'm going to." Or you can say "I'm up for the challenge," or "I bet this could be easier than I think." Or simply focus on what you do like or prefer. "Never" is a long time. Maybe you can change this phrase to "I rarely," or "I'm learning to," or even, "I'm opening to."

Your words and thoughts have great power in them. Use your power for your own good, and the good of everyone around you.

If you're like so many people, you've been taught to "get your head out of the clouds," or "be more realistic." You've probably heard people critique positive people with statements like "She's such a dreamer," or "He's not in touch with reality." I'm here to show you that you can both "be in touch with reality" and cultivate a positive mind. In essence, a positive mind is equal to a loving heart..

By cultivating a positive mind, I'm not suggesting that you stop being responsible, or that you deny that your mortgage payment is due on the first of the month or that your mother has Alzheimer's or that your kid has a drug problem, or that you're suffering from a broken heart. I'm not suggesting that you deny what's going on in the world. But I am suggesting that you can decide how you want to think and therefore how you want to feel about things that you have no control over (as well as things you do have control over).

It's important to remember that when we think or feel about something or someone, we add energy to that thing or person. Our thoughts, our words, and our emotions are energy! So even if you hear of a disaster that happened in your community, or anywhere for that matter, you can add negative energy to it by feeling horror or fear or pity or sadness, or you can add positive energy to it, by sending love to the situation or to the people involved.

Negative thoughts and emotions are not bad. They just are. They can be an alert to danger. Or a reminder of what we don't want. But when our negative thoughts and emotions take over our lives, they become a problem. They harm us, physically, because our body is so responsive to our thoughts. Excessive negative thoughts and emotions cut off the flow of creativity and solutions ("Life"). And those thoughts and feelings keep us from our Divine Purpose. Plus, excessive negativity attracts more of that negativity into our lives!

Your mind is so freaking powerful, why would you want to use it to cultivate negativity? That's like having access to the Hubble Telescope (http://hubblesite.org/) and using it to go bird watching. Or worse, not using it at all! Most of us don't access our mind's potential, in great part because we're stuck "in reality." Do you ever say "that's just the way things are"?

Well, starting right now, begin saying "I wonder if things could be different? I wonder if I could make a difference?"

If you have been cultivating a negative mind, it's likely because it's a habit for you. Maybe you learned it from your family. Or maybe you haven't given it much thought because it's so familiar. Or perhaps you think that's "just the way I am." Or you don't know how to not cultivate negativity. Or maybe you're afraid to be more positive. Well, of course I'm going to give you some exercises and some Tapping! Before I do, some quotes and some inspiration.

Epictetus was a Greek-born slave of Rome in the first century AD. He became a great philosopher and teacher and was eventually granted his freedom. Although he didn't write down his teachings, which are based in Stoic philosophy, thankfully, others did. This quote, first written in Greek, then Latin, appeared in "The Enchiridion," which was written by Arrian, a student of Epictetus: "We cannot choose our external circumstances, but we can always choose how we respond to them." That is the epitome of "cultivating a positive mind." You see, how you think about things affects how you experience things.

As Dr. Wayne Dyer said, "When we change the way we look at things, the things we look at change." If you like the way things are, then keep thinking about them the same way. If you want anything to change, then change the way you think.

One of the most basic "positive spins" on any event is for me to realize that this thing that happened is in the best interest of all concerned and that I probably have no idea "who all is concerned." There is a Divine Designer of the Universe, infinitely wise and knowing, all-seeing, all-loving. This Divine

Designer is NOT human and goes way beyond what we can imagine. If someone is suffering and is not willing to help herself out of her own suffering, then it must be a benefit to someone else or something else. She can, at some point, choose to change her circumstances by choosing new thinking. But this may never happen in this lifetime. It is difficult to wrap our relatively pea-sized minds around such a concept. But when we open our minds to Infinite Intelligence, we can begin to sense that there is so much we can't comprehend or even imagine. As you begin to cultivate a positive mind, you will open to greater and greater possibilities. When that happens, greater and greater possibilities will arrive for you. There is no end to the possibilities!

Why a positive mind? How can that help the planet & Humanity? Let's first look at why not? Negative thinking is heavy energy, a low-vibration energy. Law of Attraction will give you more heavy-energy experiences when you are on a negativity jag. Your thoughts affect the entire planet, whether you realize it or not. If you want to have a more positive effect on Humanity, you've got to cultivate a positive mind.

During the time I was writing this chapter, I experienced the following life-changing event. I was riding my bike down a steep hill in my neighborhood, zooming along, wind blowing in my hair, sun shining. It was a quiet day, mid-morning, no traffic, no people around. If I'd been unaware of my surroundings, I might have missed the woman who was lying on the sidewalk. I immediately pulled over and jumped off my bike. "Are you ok?" I asked, just getting a feel for her emotional and physical state. "I've fallen, and I can't get up." Ok, that's not verbatim what she said, but the gist of it. "I'm here to help you," I said. I then checked to see if there were any major injuries. None visible, just a skinned knee.

"I'll get behind you and lift you up," I said. I'm very strong, so I thought I'd be able to lift her. From behind, I hooked my arms under her arms. I told her to plant her feet the best she could, and then I said: "Lift." We both fell backward. It was pretty funny. I said "Let's try again," and we did. Again we fell. Next, she repositioned herself and I supported her as she got up. As she stood upright, she turned to me and gave me a huge hug. "Thank you!" she said.

I asked her name and where she lived. She still had quite a ways to walk. "Can I go get my car and drive you?" I asked. No, she assured me she was fine and wanted to walk home. She had, she said, gotten distracted by the beautiful flowers, and wasn't paying attention to where she was walking. She had tripped on a break in the sidewalk.

"Your knee is bleeding," I told her. She had Band Aids in her purse, so I put two of them on her knee. I then looked into her eyes and said, "I'm a healer. May I gently tap on you to help you recover more quickly?" She nodded.

As I gently tapped around the points, she closed her eyes, and when she opened them, her eyes looked brighter and more focused. Even a minor incident causes emotional trauma, and I wanted to help her recover and resolve this trauma right on the spot.

I then helped her on with her sun hat, handed her the walking sticks she had been carrying before the fall, gave her another hug, and sent her on her way.

From a positive perspective, I can see how this event may have seemed like a big bummer to her. But the fact that someone stopped to help her could have changed her entire outlook on her day. I know it changed mine. I had several route choices that day and had pondered which route to take on my bike, and thought it was no "mere coincidence" that I rode that way. It was my positive mind that allowed me to stop and help her. Or rather, it demanded that I stop and help her. A spark of kindness, a smile, a hand - these are the things that a positive mind contributes in the world. These are the things that can give hope. These small things can change the turn of a hundred related events.

Take a moment to think about whether or not you have been cultivating a positive mind. If you have been cultivating a positive mind, notice how that has happened, and how it affects your worldview and your reality..

If you've been stuck in a negative mindset, ask yourself why? Perhaps you are trying to cultivate positivity but are bumping up against a lifetime of negativity. Perhaps you are pretty positive about some things, but can't bring yourself to create positive thinking about others. Or maybe you feel that "People won't like me if I'm positive." You may just "not want to be positive - what's the point?" Whatever your positive mind situation is, write it down like this:

"I haven't cultivated a positive mind because____," and fill in the blank.

And guess what? We'll be using what you wrote for the Tapping protocols in this chapter!

Let's do some Tapping now for cultivating a positive mind.

Tapping on the side of the hand, say:

Even though I haven't cultivated a positive mind because _____ [fill in with your words from above], I love and accept myself

Even though I don't want to cultivate a positive mind, and you can't make me, I love and accept myself.

Even though I don't want to change my thinking, I love and accept myself

Now Tapping around the points, say these phrases:

(Top of head): I haven't cultivated a positive mind because

_____

(Inner eyebrow): I don't want to cultivate a positive mind

(Outer eye): I don't want to change my thinking

(Under eye): I don't want to change my world

(Under nose): I'm fine with the way things are now

(Chin): A positive mind is a waste of time

(Collarbone): I don't want things to change

(Under arm): I need to focus on reality

Now take a slow breath in. Exhale. That protocol was intentionally focused on the negative. Often when we do this, our mind will then argue with us, like when we said "I'm fine with the way things are" above, did you mind say "No I'm not!" or anything along those lines? That's a clue that you might be ready to change.

Notice any thoughts or images or emotions that came up for you during that tapping. Make a note of them. Use tapping to address anything that feels unresolved or irritating or "out of alignment." Did you get any "ahas" or epiphanies? Did anything come to the surface of your awareness that you've kept hidden away? Notice. Become aware.

Here is an exercise to begin cultivating a positive mind. It only takes about 10 minutes, and you can practice this every day to get deeper and deeper results.

You can choose to practice each Practice separately until you become skilled before adding the next Practice. Or you can choose to practice all three Practices each time. Whatever works for you. The key is to practice, make mistakes, notice where you made mistakes, and correct - for the deepest learning.

Practice #1 Breathing.

Sit in a comfortable place, where you can have a straight spine that isn't stiff, where you can relax and close your eyes but not fall asleep. No phone, no computer, no distractions. This can become your daily meditation practice, or you can add it to something you already do.

As you get comfortable notice your breathing. Is it shallow or deep? Is it restricted or complete? Breathing is one of the ways we bring Life Force Energy into our bodies. Life Force Energy is the Source of all that is. Breathing is the single most important thing we need to give ourselves in order to live.

Make your first intention to expand and deepen your breathing without effort, bringing in Life Force Energy in a slow, steady rhythmic way. "Slow breathing" is a good way to get there. Often we gulp in a big deep breath, but it's time to learn to take in slow breaths that fill your lungs and continue on down to your solar plexus and then to your gut and belly. Then breathe down even further - into your pelvic bowl. And finally, breathe down your legs and to your feet.

Practice this each day until it becomes easy for you. Then begin to practice it when you are not in your comfortable place. Practice it at work, in the car, at the grocery store, when you talk to your kids and your spouse. And ultimately, you want to begin to practice this when you are uncomfortable or angry or frightened or feeling defensive. If every person on the planet learned this simple technique, there would be way fewer conflicts, because bringing attention to your breathing automatically takes your attention away from your anger or fear, and calms down your nervous system so that you can think in a conscious way.

Practice #2 Feelings & Sensations.

As you get comfortable in your sitting position, and you've smoothed your breathing to a slow, deep, steady rhythm, begin to take notice of any sensations in your body. Mentally scan your body, from the top of your head, down your face and ears, down to your chin and neck, then to your shoulders. Notice any tightness, pain, discomfort, or other sensations. Bring your breath to any place that has a sensation. Continue your mental scan - down your back, noticing the vertebrae of your spine. Scan down the front of your torso - from your clavicle, down to your abdomen, include your hips and your hip flexors. If there is any discomfort, send your breath there.

Take another scan down the interior of your torso, noticing your organs, your heart, your lungs, your liver and spleen, your kidneys, your digestive system, your ovaries, your genitals. Send breath to any organ or any place inside you that feels uncomfortable. This should be done as slowly and deliberately as possible. You are sending Life Force Energy directly to any part of you that is lacking this energy.

Discomfort and disease are results of a lack of Life Force Energy. And that happens when we ignore our body, when we let our mind run away with us into negativity. Life Force Energy is a positive force. Consciously bring more of it into your body!

As you become more practiced at noticing the sensations in your body, and at bringing Life Force Energy to those sensations, learn to do this when you are at work or driving your car or talking to your best friend. Learn to do it when you are at a party. You will discover how much your thoughts and reactions are in response to a negative sensation in your body, and that the feeling is an old habit. Learn to breathe into your sensations when you are at your most uncomfortable, and notice how much more empowered you begin to feel.

Practice #3 Thoughts.

Now that you've practiced and become more adept at breathing and are consciously breathing in Life Force Energy more and more of the time, and now that you've become more and more aware of the sensations in your body, it's time to add in your thoughts to the mix. To become more conscious of your thoughts and how your thoughts are controlling you.

Research has shown that humans think on average of 75,000 thoughts per day. We talked about this in Chapter 4. The majority of these thoughts are coming from the subconscious mind, are habitual, repetitive, and mostly negative. That's a lot of thought power going to negative things.

Next time you're with other people, pay close attention to what happens when the conversation goes negative, as it eventually will. Watch the person talking as she sinks into her "story." By story I don't mean the narrative, but rather, the emotional attachment to telling the story and gaining approval or inclusion from others. You can see her go into a trance-like state. She's talking and probably quite animated. But her eyes have glazed over somewhat, and she isn't really thinking. She's reacting. Her fight-or-flight response is clicked on. And if you offer something like a positive thought or idea, she's likely to shoot you a look or get defensive.

Now notice when *you* do it. When you go into a trance created by the sound of your own voice in your head. It's way more common than you realize. You may not notice it until you've stopped talking. Just breathe. If you notice your own trance state while you're talking, try slowing your speech or take a deep breath mid-sentence. Or stop when you get to the end of a sentence (even if you think you have more to say) and let others speak.

This practice will build your self-confidence and esteem. You will find that people are more attracted to you. And you may influence others.

These are three very simple, very powerful practices for self-empowerment. And that's good for the planet

Here is some Tapping is for those who really do want to cultivate a positive mind.

Tapping on the side of the hand, say these phrases:

Even though I haven't known how to cultivate a positive mind, I love and accept myself

Even though I haven't been aware of how powerful a positive mind might be, I love and accept myself

Even though I haven't cultivated a positive mind, I'm ready to begin to cultivate a positive mind now

Now tapping around the points:

(Top of head): I haven't cultivated a positive mind

(Inner eyebrow): I wasn't aware of cultivating a positive mind

(Outer eye): I haven't known how to do it

(Under eye): But now I'm ready

(Under nose): To cultivate a positive mind

(Chin): Becoming aware is a big step

(Collarbone): Making a decision is another big step

(Under arm): I'm deciding to cultivate a positive mind

(Top of head): A positive mind takes cultivation

(Inner eyebrow): Planting the seed

(Outer eye): Giving it what it needs to grow

(Under eye): Keeping the weeds of negativity under control

(Under nose): Allowing the positive mind to sprout

(Chin): To grow

(Collarbone): To flourish

(Under arm): And harvesting the fruit

(Top of head): It doesn't have to be difficult

(Inner eyebrow): It doesn't have to be hard work

(Outer eye): But it does take attention

(Under eye): Practice

(Under nose): Allowing mistakes

(Chin): More practice

(Collarbone): Noticing my progress

(Under arm): And ongoing practice

Take a deep breath. You can tap more and add anything you feel compelled to add about how you'd like it to be to cultivate a positive mind.

And this Tapping is for those who have already cultivated a somewhat positive mind and want to expand that.

Tapping on the side of the hand point, say these phrases:

Even though I've been cultivating a positive mind, I still find myself in a negative place sometimes, and I love and accept myself anyway

Even though I've been leaning towards a positive mind, I find myself unconsciously going negative, and I love and accept myself

Even though I've been fairly positive, I'd like to enhance my positive mind

(Top of head): I'm ready to more deeply cultivate my positive mind

(Inner eyebrow): I don't need to be perfect at it

(Outer eye): But I'd like to have fewer negative thoughts and emotions

(Under eye): I'd like for negative thoughts to leave me more quickly

(Under nose): I'd like to not get caught up in other people's negativity

(Chin): I'm choosing now to become more aware of my mind state

(Collarbone): More of the time

(Under arm): And practice cultivating a more positive mind

Take a deep breath. It's as simple as becoming aware of your mental, emotional, and physical state in any given moment. Simple, but not so easy. Especially if you've spent a lifetime avoiding those feelings. Cultivating a positive mind is NOT about stuffing your negative emotions. It's about noticing your emotions, and if they are negative, resolving them or completing them.

Cultivating a positive mind is one of the most powerful things you can do to affect your own inner world, and the outer world around you.

#7 DISCOVER YOUR UNIQUE GIFTS. USE AND SHARE THEM GENEROUSLY!

*"Today you are You, that is truer than true.
There is no one alive who is Youer than You."*

~Dr. Seuss

You have a unique set of gifts and talents. Everyone does. Your Soul has a specific purpose for being in this physically manifested body at this time in human history. Think about that. Your Soul decided to come here in this lifetime, be born to your family, and have the experiences you've had. All so that you could wake up one day (today would be a good day!) and realize that Life isn't happening *to* you, it's happening *for* you.

Your Soul has things to learn and discover, things to share. Your gifts are perfectly suited to your Soul's Purpose, and to the things you need to learn and discover and share. If you are feeling unsatisfied in any area of your life, the answer to your dilemma is within these ideas. And when you discover the solution, you will be changing your world for the better.

And when you change your world for the better, you change the whole world for the better. That's why I encourage you to focus on what you're for, not what you're against (see Chapter 4). It does no good to spend your time and energy and power focusing on what you're against. So if, for example, you're against people suffering from hunger, be for feeding and nourishing all.

DISCOVER YOUR UNIQUE GIFTS

So what are your unique gifts? Gifts are the things you do innately - you are drawn to do them, to get better at them, to gain mastery of them. You probably knew the essence of your gifts when you were quite young. Maybe you cared for all the dolls and stuffed animals.. Maybe you ran a lemonade stand. Maybe you liked to draw or paint. Maybe you saw angels. Maybe you took apart your bike and put it back together again in a new way. Perhaps you spent hours throwing a baseball or kicking a soccer ball or passing a lacrosse ball. Did you love to play the piano or the violin or the guitar? Were you the best marble player in the neighborhood? Did you love to read? Make up stories? Take photographs? Dance?

Your gifts aren't necessarily the things that you did, but the reasons you did them. For example, if your were rarely seen without a basketball, and you loved playing basketball, your gift might be that you are a world-class basketball player. Or, your gifts might be team-building, coaching, seeing the big picture, excellent hand-eye coordination, or any of a number of other gifts that are utilized when playing basketball.

If you were fortunate, someone noticed your gifts and encouraged you and helped you develop them. But my experience is that most young people don't receive that kind of mentorship. Too many parents and teachers think that gifts are genius. That gifts don't require practice. That gifts mean the child is perfect at something. And too many adults are too quick to give up on children because their gifts are of the more subtle nature, or they don't align with the adult's ideas of what talent and giftedness is.

And that's where you come in.

If you were like me growing up, no one really noticed your gifts, or if they did, they didn't recognize them as gifts. I spent my formative years jumping from thing to thing, never being encouraged to practice or get good at anything. I grew up with the implied message that if I wasn't innately good at something, I shouldn't bother to pursue it. And I know I'm not the only one who got this message. Many people tell me similar stories, like it wasn't ok to make mistakes or fail. And so they decided they weren't good at anything, or just plain weren't good enough. These are the people who come to me feeling unfulfilled and knowing there is something more calling them.

Let's change that thinking starting right now! Making mistakes and failing is an essential part of learning and growing. I certainly wasn't taught that. Were you?

Over the course of my life, I pursued more than one career that I was good at, but that I wasn't gifted at. So I lacked the passion, the desire, and the perseverance to improve my performance, and I felt dissatisfied. I used to feel as though I'd wasted all that time, but now I see how much I've learned from trying to be someone I'm not, and pursuing something because other people thought I should. I also suffered from trauma, shame, and low self-esteem, so it's not surprising that I sabotaged myself along the way.

Take some time now to begin to rediscover the innate gifts you came into this life with. Begin to notice the life situations your Soul brought you to. What could you be needing to learn? Life hasn't been happening to you, but rather, for you. Even if you were a victim as a child, and even if you've been a victim until now, you can choose to no longer be a victim, but rather to see the gifts in those experiences. Are you strong? Thoughtful? Creative? Did you develop these characteristics (or some other ones) because of your situation? Your Soul knew what you needed in order to learn. Your Soul was NOT needing to learn to be a victim. But possibly compassion for those who are victims, or those who victimize. Only YOU can know for sure.

I encourage you to do some journaling about this. There is great freedom in discovering your unique gifts, your powers - especially if they've been hiding. Go ahead now and begin to get this down on paper. Start your Unique Gifts list. Write about the things you've done in your life when you've felt fully engaged, fully satisfied. Mentally scan your life from early childhood to the present. Often our gifts show up in some form early in our lives. And remember that "unique" doesn't mean that no one else does what you do. It means that you bring something special to it that no one else brings.

Also write about times when someone squashed your gifts - maybe someone said "you're not very good at that," or "don't bother," or "you can't make money doing that!" or worse. Especially if your gifts go against the norm in your family, your culture, your circle. Remember back to when you were a child and someone told you to stop doing what you love? Do you remember how much that hurt? It hurt because you knew better, but you felt you had to listen.

My own paternal grandfather was an incredibly talented artist. He created jewelry boxes and pitchers and lamp shades out of copper. The detail and quality of his work was stunning. I still have some of his pieces. But his family, including my grandmother, did not encourage his passion. To them, it was a waste of time. When my mother married my father and met my grandfather, she encouraged his artistic abilities. But by then my grandfather had become pretty wretched. He was an alcoholic, but had stopped drinking using pure willpower. That's a miserable way to stop drinking. He was a miserable man. If only someone had encouraged his gifts earlier in life!

During the times you've felt satisfied, what activity were you engaged in? What skills were you using? In what ways did this feel satisfying? This is Soul Satisfaction, and each of us will be profoundly changing the world when we spend more time feeling Soul Satisfied.

You probably have many things to put on your Unique Gifts list. You might feel satisfied when you are swimming, or building a computer, or teaching, or raising kids, or cooking, or running a company, or helping people in need, or reading a book, or walking on the beach, or writing stories, or taking photographs, or riding a bike, or rebuilding an engine, or...whatever it is, write it down.

You don't need to be good at it for it to be on your list. In fact, you might not be good at it yet, but you still enjoy it.

I felt powerless as a child, and frustrated. And as I grew, I tried to express my power. I discovered that some people were intimidated by me. I was sometimes called "bossy" as a teen, trying to find my power. Others called me a leader. It was confusing to be intimidating and feel so insecure inside. I discovered later in life that my Soul came here to learn personal empowerment - neither powerlessness or overpowering, but a balance, which I've come to call "Dynamic Equilibrium." I can be myself, stand in my power, speak my truth, and not need to be right. One of my unique gifts is cultivating personal power - in myself and in others who ask me for help.

I also went back to my childhood to discover that I've always loved doing puzzles - especially jigsaw puzzles. Seeing the pieces all laid out on the table, and putting them together to make a beautiful image. Creating wholeness. This particular gift has served me well in business - seeing the big picture and bringing all the parts together to create it; and in my coaching practice, using Tapping to help people collect up the "splintered parts" of their energetic and emotional body, and return to wholeness.

Your gifts are often hiding behind your skills. You're good at something, so you pursue it, when really it doesn't fulfill you. If you were brought up to believe that you shouldn't pursue something unless you're already good at it, you may have suffered from this. If this is your current situation, I encourage you to find ways to bring your greatest gifts into your work. When you do, you'll feel more fulfilled, and there's a good chance you will be more successful.

And your greatest gift of all may still be hiding. We tend to hide our greatest gifts where no one can find them (not even us) - behind our greatest fear. This is an ancient mechanism for keeping us safe. Our tribal ancestors would die if they were ostracized from the tribal group. If we were different or too smart, we would be kicked out of the tribe. Interestingly, that is still the case. The difference now is that we can easily find a new tribe today. Don't let your friends and family's judgment of you hold you back from sharing your greatest gifts! The world needs you!

For me, the earliest memory of a gift that I have is from Kindergarten. In my class, we used those half-pint milk cartons - the kind we got with school lunch - with the tops cut off, filled with soil. We planted nasturtium seeds and in a few days, the seeds sprouted. I still remember the amazing feeling of cultivating plant life. I was in awe. I took that little plant home and transplanted it into the garden, where it flourished and flowered. I have been a gardener ever since. I have created some amazing gardens over the years, including nasturtiums from seed whenever possible - as a nod to my earliest experience with gardening.

I expanded my love for gardening to create some lovely outdoor spaces over the years. Not just to experience the beauty, but for the satisfaction of cultivation - seeing things grow and bloom and return year after year, or only stay for a season. I love seeing the palette that nature creates with. I've moved several times, and I was able to learn about the climate and soil conditions of the place I was living at the time by the types of plants that thrived there. I've lived in the tropics, where things grow green and large and fast and have blooms that smell heavenly on a warm evening. I've lived in the Pacific Northwest, where everything from pines to roses to strawberries to green beans to ferns grow hardy and thrive through the wonderfully mild seasons. I've lived on the East Coast of the United States, where weather is more severe, and totally different varieties prosper. I've lived where the soil is sandy, where it's rich and loamy, where it's rocky. When I've lived in small apartments, I've cultivated house plants, or created a patio garden. And now, living in my Airstream Motor

Home, I have cultivated an outdoor garden along the side of where my rig is parked.

What I've learned from all this gardening is that I love the art of cultivating. And that I have a gift for it. I seem to be able to whisper to plants and understand them. I can group a variety of plants that will grow well and flourish together. I can cultivate an environment that is both water efficient and lush. I have always seemed to have an innate relationship with plants and how to help them grow as individuals, while creating a beautiful garden.

When I was an Executive Manager, I discovered that I was equally able to work with employees - helping the individuals to grow, while cultivating a cohesive team. As with gardening, team-building requires an innate understanding of lots of types of people and how they are similar and different. How they work well together, and which things should be left out of the team garden.

And now, as a Woman of Wisdom, and Personal Transformation Specialist, I've created a practice where I cultivate the greatest version of individuals, groups and organizations, while cultivating my own thriving business. Cultivation is the common key. Cultivation is my gift. I am now cultivating new ideas about healing, and how to take Tapping to as many people as possible during my lifetime. I plant the seeds of inspiration, healing, and resolution in fertile soil, and nurture them, and allow them to grow. I feel fulfilled on a daily basis.

Wouldn't you like to use your gifts to help others and feel fulfilled? It doesn't have to be for business. Perhaps you use your gifts as a hobby. Or in your volunteer situations. Or maybe you simply wait for opportunities to share your gifts in your community.

Tapping protocol to discover your unique gifts.

Let's do some Tapping to help you discover your unique gifts. Or to reaffirm them if you're already aware of them. Set an intention for this Tapping. Something like: "I feel a calling and I want to answer it. Help me, Universe, to discover my calling." Or, "Help me to discover greater and greater ways to share my gifts - for the highest good of all." You can word your intention in whatever way suits you.

Sit quietly, in a comfortable position. Back straight, but not stiff. Head up. Shoulders back to keep your chest open. Breathe deeply three times before beginning.

Pay attention to whatever thoughts, images, memories or sensations arise for you as you tap. These are clues from your subconscious mind or from the Infinite Mind. Stop and acknowledge them or write them down. Or you can simply tap the whole protocol before stopping to check in.

Tapping around the points, beginning at the top of the head:

(Top of head) - Maybe I have some unique gifts
(Inner eyebrow) - I never really thought it was possible
(Outer eye) - I'm open to discovering them, even though I'm not sure what they are
(Under eye) - Maybe my unique gifts are so close to me
(Under nose) - That I haven't been able to see them or recognize them
(Chin) - Maybe my unique gifts seem "normal" to me
(Collarbone) - But what if they really are special

(Under arm) - I'm open to discovering my greatest gifts

(Top of head) - Maybe I've been hiding my gifts away
(Inner eyebrow) - Keeping them safe from criticism
(Outer eye) - Perhaps it's time to uncover my gifts?
(Under eye) - For myself and for others
(Under nose) - What if I can be of service?
(Chin) - What if I can inspire others?
(Collarbone) - What if my gifts really are special?
(Under arm) - I'm open to discovering my greatest gifts

Take a deep breath and check in with what cam up while you tapped. Did you notice any sensations in your body? Did you receive any inspirations? Were you aware of any thoughts or memories - whether they seemed related to this topic or not?

You can use this Tapping protocol as often as you like for inspiration. I'm convinced that many of us have not yet discovered what will be the greatest gift of all.

Tapping protocol for inspiration.

In this next protocol, you will hopefully find inspiration to use your gifts in the Service of the Divine, and for the Greater Good. Even if you help one other person, you are positively impacting the world. We never know how far the ripple effect will go.

Again, pay attention to whatever thoughts, images, memories or sensations arise for you as you tap. These are clues from your subconscious mind or from the Infinite Mind. Stop and acknowledge them or write them down. Or you can simply tap the whole protocol before stopping to check in.

Tapping around the points, beginning at the top of the head, use these phrases, one phrase at each Tapping point:

(Top of head) - I know I have some very unique gifts

(Inner eyebrow) - I've been denying them

(Outer eye) Hiding my gifts away from the world

(Under eye) It's feels scary to show my gifts

(Under nose) People might not approve

(Chin) People might criticize or reject me

(Collarbone) And these gifts are my greatest treasures

(Under arm) Maybe I should just keep my gifts safely tucked away

(Top of head) I wonder why God gave me these unique gifts

(Inner eyebrow) If I'm supposed to keep them hidden out of sight

(Outer eye) It doesn't feel right to deny my gifts

(Under eye) But it's scary to show them to the world

(Under nose) I wonder if it's possible that I've been given these gifts for a reason

(Chin) A reason that is greater than me

(Collarbone) Maybe these gifts are meant to help or inspire others?

(Under arm) Maybe I could share my gifts out in the world?

(Top of head) Who would care about my very unique gifts?

(Inner eyebrow) Why would anyone be interested?

(Outer eye) I don't see how I could possibly help or inspire others

(Under eye) But maybe that's just my limited thinking?

(Under nose) I've certainly been inspired by others

(Chin) I've been helped by others

(Collarbone) People are waiting to know my gifts and hear my message

(Under arm) People are waiting for me to bring my gifts forward

Take a deep breath and check in with what cam up while you tapped. Did you notice any sensations in your body? Did you receive any inspirations? Were you aware of any thoughts or memories - whether they seemed related to this topic or not?

You can journal about this, or you may be inspired to take action right now. Or maybe you still want to sit with this idea. Whatever comes up for you is okay.

Where else might your gifts be hiding?

In my work as a Coach and Personal Transformation Specialist, I work with lots of people who have very different life experiences. Many of my clients have suffered greatly from childhood abuse, traumatic experiences, and great loss. As we work together and resolve those issues, it is almost a certainty that they will discover something wonderful that has come to them from having experienced the suffering and survived.

Manure is a great fertilizer. Compost is a great fertilizer. As in our garden, the shit that happens in our lives can be used to cultivate our gifts. If we let it. Trauma usually needs to be resolved for the greatest results, but, as you may have guessed by now, working with a skilled Tapping practitioner, one can resolve old trauma permanently.

What stories to you tell yourself about your past? Do you hinder yourself because you were abused? I used to wonder who I'd be if I'd been loved and supported as a child in the way I had wanted. I was sure that my relationships would have been better if I'd received affection and encouragement. And this may have been true to some extent. But once all that stuff was resolved in me, these stories were now simply excuses. Once I became aware that I was making excuses, I decided to take responsibility for my life, and I was able to really move forward.

Yes, there are exceptions, but for the most part, I have seen and worked with people who experienced what I would say are "way worse" events in their lives, have resolved those events and discovered some amazing inspiration and motivation to change the world.

Use your gifts.

Imagine if everyone on the planet, each and every one of the 7.5 Billion of us humans, used our greatest gifts and unique talents in service to Humanity and the planet. What if people stopped trying to be someone they're not - in order to please others or gain power, recognition and material wealth? Imagine if people learned how to deeply love themselves, and practiced it every day!

Now don't get me wrong - there's nothing wrong with recognition and material wealth, but when those are the motives for one's actions, it is a guarantee that many people will suffer. On the other hand, when we set out with the intention of being truly authentic, and of using our gifts in service to Humanity, if we open our hearts and help ourselves and others, we will have an amazing impact. Money and wealth will be magnetized to us Others may still suffer as a result, but if our intention is to help and be of service, the suffering of others becomes their responsibility.

It is not antithetical to be of service and have great wealth. Our Western culture tends to say it's not okay to be of service and have wealth, but that is a huge misperception. Look at Oprah Winfrey. Look at Joel Osteen. Consider Deepak Chopra, or Eckhart Tolle, or Michael Beckwith. Even Mother Teresa, though she chose to live an austere life, was able to raise millions of dollars for her charity work.

Think of just one famous Billionaire, and how much impact that person could have if she realigned her priorities for the Greatest Good of Humanity and the Planet. What about a large corporation - not a human, but a business! Imagine if a company like Exxon Mobile rallied it's resources and changed the direction of the corporation to serve the greatest good of all, including our Earth? What these corporations fail to see is that doing so would, in the long run, have the greatest impact on profits as well.

I know I'm dreaming, but when I sense into those ideas, it feels so amazing. I feel hopeful and lighthearted and inspired! I know it won't happen where everyone is doing their inner work and using their gifts. But I know we can each aim for that in our own lives - to use our greatest gifts and unique talents in service to the Greatest Good of Humanity and the planet, to stop trying to be someone we're not, and to deeply love ourselves.

Your greatest gifts and unique talents - you may be underestimating yourself!

Each of us has at least one unique gift or talent. You may have forgotten what yours is, or you may be using yours every day. Or maybe you sometimes use your gifts and talents, but mostly you work at a job that is boring and soul-sucking.

Sit quietly for a few minutes with your pen and journal. When you imagine yourself doing something really outrageously wonderful, what do you see yourself doing? For this exercise, imagine yourself giving a TED Talk, or a presentation to a group of like-minded people. What would you be talking about? Now imagine taking that topic to a group of dissimilar thinkers. How will you present your topic in a way that actually engages them and doesn't alienate or repel?

If you are a creative, imagine yourself doing your creative work and having a huge impact on Humanity. What are you doing in this vision? How are you sharing your creativity? Who are you attracting into your life? Who are you collaborating with?

If you are an inventor or a philosopher, what is your greatest impact? Sit quietly and ask for inspiration.

How can you begin using your greatest gifts now? What small step can you take towards your greatest impact? Notice any resistance you feel about this. We are, all of us, living tiny versions of our individual and collective potential. It's scary to step out of the box we've put ourselves in. It's frightening to be different and to be bold.

Of course we'll do some Tapping on that!

Sense into the resistance or fear you feel as you think about actualizing the vision you have for yourself. Where do you feel it in your body? Your heart? Your lungs? Your head? Your gut? Or somewhere else? Become aware of the sensation. Breathe into it. How intense is it, on a scale of 1-10? What does the sensation "look" like? What size and shape is the sensation? What color is it?

Now, Tapping around the points, say these phrases. Stop after each phrase to see if you get an image, a thought, or if the sensation changes.

(Top of head) - This sensation
(Pause and reflect while still Tapping on the top of your head)
(Inner eyebrow) - What if I were to actualize this vision?
(Pause and reflect while still Tapping on your inner eyebrow)
(Outer eye) - I'm comfortable where I am
(Pause and reflect while still Tapping on your outer eye)
(Under eye) - And yet I'm feeling called to do something greater
(Pause and reflect while still Tapping on your under eye)
(Under nose) - I feel resistance
(Pause and reflect while still Tapping on your under nose)
(Chin) - I feel this sensation
(Pause and reflect while still Tapping on your chin)
(Collarbone) - I'm experiencing new insights
(Pause and reflect while still Tapping on your collarbones)
(Under arm) - I'm choosing to pay attention

Now, take a deep breath in and out. Reflect on any insights you may have had. You may have discovered a deeper layer that needs additional Tapping. You can do this on your own. Simply focus on one thing - a thought or a sensation, and start Tapping around the points. What's coming up now? No matter where your mind leads you, trust it and follow along. There will probably be a point at which you feel like you can't go any further with Tapping, and yet you sense you're not deep enough. This is when you will want to get help. I recommend finding an experienced Tapping practitioner to work with.

KNOW WHO YOU ARE, BE WHO YOU ARE...IN EVERYTHING YOU DO

As you may have noticed, every chapter in this book is leading you to one main thing:

To be the best and most authentic version of yourself, and to love and accept everything about yourself - even the stuff you don't like.

In order to do this, you will need to let go of all the things that aren't truly you. This requires "unlearning" and letting go. Think on that for a moment. Do you have beliefs that you didn't even choose for yourself? Of course you do. Family, society, culture, religion all impose their beliefs on us when we're small. Most of us had no way to say, "No, that doesn't feel right for me." And so that belief that didn't feel right as a kid likely became an unconscious habit.

As you've begun to take the steps in this book, hopefully you've discovered new perspectives. Not my perspectives, but your own authentic perspectives. As you've started to stop judging yourself and others, you may have discovered a new acceptance, tolerance, compassion. Not to "put up with" actions and behaviors of others that cross your boundaries, but rather, to meet others "where they are," and to know that where they are isn't where you are.

Here's one way to shift your perspective a bit. Think of a divisive issue that you feel passionately about. Ask yourself this question: "What would it take for someone on the other side of this issue to convince me to switch sides?" If your answer is something like, "There's no way they could convince me to switch sides," then ask yourself, "Why would I think I can convince them to switch sides." You have to meet people where they are and find common ground. Not try to jump the chasm that exists and try to drag them across it.

So if you can let go of trying to convince others to think just like you, you will begin to find freedom. When you let go of the need to be right, you will experience miracles. When you find your authentic self and begin to truly live your authentic self, you will allow others to do the same. Finding your unique gifts and sharing them, and allowing others to find theirs and share theirs will have a huge impact on Humanity.

#8 HEAL YOURSELF

"The practice of forgiveness is our most important
contribution to the healing of the world."

~Marianne Williamson

When I say "Heal Yourself," I'm talking about your physical, emotional, mental, and spiritual self. Truly holistic healing. You are capable of moving toward greater wholeness in each of these areas. If you leave out one of these categories, your life will be out of balance, your experience as a human won't be as rich as it can be, and the world's holistic healing will be hindered. Let's take a brief look at what's involved in each of these areas, how you can begin to heal (get back to wholeness), and how your healing affects others..

Physical health includes your current physical body, and all that it represents. Healing your physical self means taking charge of your healing, not giving your power away to doctors and practitioners. It means questioning diagnosis and treatments, getting other opinions, and knowing that YOU have the final say in your health care. This is particularly important these days. Physical health means asking questions about your medications until you get all the answers you need. It means working out a plan with your practitioner to get off your meds, if possible, not just a plan to get on them.

Not everyone can be perfectly healthy. The goal here is to take notice of your body and what it's trying to tell you. The human body is not separate from the mind. They work in tandem. This cannot be overstated. Whatever your mind holds, your body projects. This includes your conscious mind and your subconscious mind. Your body is a powerful communication device. Your body never betrays you. Your body reflects what your conscious and unconscious minds are "thinking" and believing. Your body is a servant to your mind. It is capable of letting itself die to honor what the mind is projecting.

Please don't interpret this to mean that your illnesses are your fault, or that you wanted to get sick or injured. It rarely works this way (though sometimes it does). Have you ever had a dream and tried to interpret it? Your dreams are a mental manifestation of your conscious and subconscious thoughts, your beliefs, and your experiences. Your physical body is a physical manifestation of your conscious and subconscious thoughts, your beliefs, and your experiences.

Dreams rarely are linear or literal. In dreams, our thoughts are delivered to us through metaphors, images, puns, synonyms and other cryptic forms. Let's say, for example, you have a dream where you are running down a rocky road, and a dinosaur is chasing you. You can't seem to get away, and it feels like you are running in place. Suddenly, the rocky road turns to wet cement and you are slogging along. How would you interpret that dream? Dreams are your subconscious mind processing thoughts, events, and emotions, and the subconscious mind isn't logical. It can't communicate in full sentences. Thus the cryptic messages. You have to learn to interpret your own dreams.

Well, our bodies communicate in the same way. When you were a baby, you responded to whatever your body communicated to you. If you were hungry, you cried or screamed until you were fed. If you felt anxious (and no, you didn't really know you felt anxious, but you were out of alignment, you were uncomfortable), again you cried or screamed. If you were lucky, someone comforted you and soothed you until you calmed down. If you were less fortunate, someone may have gotten upset with you and made you feel worse. If you sensed discord in your surroundings, you cried. And again, hopefully someone comforted you. But it is actually more likely that you weren't soothed, and therefore you learned to accept your discomfort.

As you grew, the people around you were likely less and less sympathetic to your needs and discomforts, and way less sympathetic to your reactions. Rather than teach you about your emotions and feelings, maybe they said things like "Be a big girl," or "Boys don't cry," or, "I'll give you something to cry about." Or perhaps they just said "You don't need to feel bad," or "There's nothing to cry about." And then maybe they even labeled you in some way... "needy," "pain in the ass," "too sensitive," "big baby," "wimp." It was at this point when you began to stop trusting your body's messages. Soon, you learned to stuff away your feelings, and you likely forgot that your body ever communicated to you. And maybe you began to feel like your body betrayed you.

But I promise you, your body never betrayed you. On the contrary, our amazing bodies are in service to our minds. If, for example, you learned that it wasn't safe to say "no," and now you are still afraid to say "no," but you want to say "no," your body will eventually say "no" for you. It will break down, or get sick, or worse, so that you can say no like you wanted to in the first place, and do so without fear or guilt. "No, I can't go to that event, I'm in too much pain."

So in order to be at your best health, you've got to be your authentic self. Otherwise, your mind will constantly be giving your body information and signals that go against your natural flow. Balance in mental health, emotional health, and spiritual health are all part of excellent physical health. A holistic approach yields the best results.

When you are at your vibrant best in your physical health, you radiate self-confidence, self-love, personal power. When you take excellent care of your body temple, you will likely be more respected at work and in your profession. You attract people to you. People want to know you, to know how you stay so vibrant, to hear what you have to say. When you are at your best health, you can have a profound effect on the planet, simply by your being.

And it's important to note here that physical health is not a stand-alone. Some people focus solely on physical health and financial wealth and totally avoid emotions and spirit. Generally speaking, this leads to deep dissatisfaction. But when we add in a spiritual practice such as meditation or yoga and Tapping, the fulfillment becomes much more well-rounded.

This is one of my favorite ways to Tap for Physical Health. It is like praying and giving gratitude and appreciation all in one protocol. In these rounds, we use statements of our desired outcome. This may bring up some resistance, and that resistance is tappable. Make notes of anything that comes up for you as you tap these rounds.

I recommend a short "Daily Tapping" practice. This should not be a burden for you or else you're not likely to do it. Get into the habit of Tapping while you drive (with your eyes open of course!), while you're riding the train or bus, or as an add-on to your daily meditation practice. Even one round of Tapping a couple of times a day will begin to make a big difference in the way you feel. This list that you're creating can be used to focus your Tapping. Or you can tap on whatever is coming up for you at any time. Remember, we are not trying to fix anything, but rather to release what isn't truly part of our authentic self.. You may discover too, that as you tap, your subconscious mind gives you clues as to what you need to do to create these healthy situations. For example, as you tap, your mind may give you a clue about "more movement" for better health, or it may just give you the word "iron," or "spinach" which contains iron. When you then Google 'iron deficiency," the symptoms may match how you've been feeling. **DO NOT** use this as a replacement for your medical care, but rather, inner guidance for what to ask your healthcare professional about.

Tapping for physical health.

Tapping around the points, beginning at the top of the head:

(Top of head) Thank you body,
(Inner eyebrow) For keeping my heart beating
(Outer eye) And thank you body,
(Under eye) For keeping my lungs breathing

(Under nose) And for all the millions of things you do
(Chin) To keep me alive and healthy
(Collar bone) I could never keep track of it all
(Under arm) You are totally amazing, body!

(Top of head) Thank you body,
(Inner eyebrow) For maintaining my vibrant health
(Outer eye) For balancing my hormones
(Under eye) For regulating my blood pressure
(Under nose) Thank you body for craving healthy foods
(Chin) And for maintaining my ideal weight
(Collar bone) I'm learning to listen to you, body
(Under arm) And to respond to your needs

(Top of head) I'm paying better attention, body
(Inner eyebrow) To the messages you give me
(Outer eye) I've taken you for granted
(Under eye) But now I see things differently
(Under nose) Thank you body for supporting me
(Chin) And for carrying me through life
(Collar bone) I really do appreciate you, body
(Under arm) I want us both to be happy

Take a deep breath. Really feel your body, your cells, your muscles. Feel into the appreciation for everything your body does for you. You can always add to these Tapping rounds with things that are specific to you. If you're sick, thank your body for creating wellness. If you're in pain, thank your body for alleviating the pain. Thank your body for what you want, as if you already have it. Tap while you say these appreciations. Do this every day and notice how your body responds.

If body weight is a problem for you.

If you've ever tried to get to your ideal body weight, you know that "diets" don't work. The weight-loss industry is a multi-billion dollar industry in the U.S. alone. The success rate of the weight loss industry isn't advertised, but it is very low. People keep hoping that the next thing will solve their weight problem, once and for all. What the weight-loss industry doesn't tell you is that getting to ideal body weight isn't just about the food. It isn't just "eat less, exercise more." If it were, we'd be able to easily solve the obesity epidemic.

There are emotional components to weight that are rarely addressed. These emotional components are stress, anxiety, trauma, abuse, limiting beliefs, peer pressure, family systems, just to name a few. I tell you this not to make you feel hopeless, but rather, to give you hope. Remember when you were a kid and you played a game called "hotter/colder"? Someone would hide an object, and someone else would begin searching for it. As the person got closer to the object, the hider would say "hotter!" And as the searcher got farther away from the object, the hider would say "colder!" Without the clues, it would have been very difficult for the searcher. Almost impossible.

Your body is giving you "hotter" and "colder" clues to what it needs and what you need. It communicates through sensations, cravings, emotions, and images in your mind. Are you listening? Are you honoring your body? Do you trust your body? If your body is telling you to change something, be open to listening and changing. There is a saying that is often used in AA: "Doing the same things over and over and expecting different results is the definition of insanity."

Shows like "The Biggest Loser" don't pay attention to the contestant's emotional issues and patterns. I've watched that show a few times, and right from the beginning, I'm thinking, "She has a habit of going through the drive-through at a fast-food place whenever she's upset or bored. If they don't help her with that, she doesn't have a chance! You've got to replace that habit with something more appealing!" But they don't. They take the contestant away from her normal surroundings and train her hard. She has coaches and doctors and nutritionists. She loses the weight and gets in shape, but when she goes back home, she's triggered by all the old familiar sights, sounds, and activities. And now she's alone without her trainers, and with no emotional tools. If only she had had Tapping, she might have a chance!

If you struggle with ideal body weight - whatever that is for you, not what it is to the media, try these two simple Tapping routines:

Routine #1 to begin to trust your body around eating.

Begin using this protocol with a meal you've already prepared, but haven't yet begun to eat. Let's say, for this example, that you have made a plate of pasta with cream sauce, a slice of garlic bread, and a salad. On the side you have a glass of red wine.

It's important to notice your body as you do this protocol. Your body wants you to listen and develop trust.

Looking at your meal, Tap around the points like this, using words that describe what you are actually planning to eat:

(Top of head) This food looks so good!
(Inner eyebrow) This food smells so good!

(Outer eye) The pasta with cream sauce has got me salivating (again, really notice your body and what it's telling you. It will communicate to you through sensations, thoughts, and images).

(Under eye) The portion looks just right

(Notice if your body agrees with you, or says something like "too much," or "we'd be fine with half that," or even "not enough food there."

(Under nose) The salad looks so fresh

(Chin) I'm looking forward to eating all this food

(Collar bone) The glass of wine is just the right touch

(Under arm) Thank you, Universe, for this amazing meal

The first time you do this, you may notice strong sensations. You may notice nothing. But I encourage you to do this before every meal or snack. At the very least, it will postpone eating for 15 seconds, which will calm your system. It will also get you aligned with your food, making it easier for your body to make the most of what you eat. You can do this Tapping silently if you wish, but out loud when you're alone is very powerful.

Routine #2 to let your body know what you desire.

Whenever you are aware of your body, do this simple protocol to let your body know that you trust it to attain and maintain your healthy body weight. In addition to other benefits, you will stop mentally beating yourself up.

(Top of head) Thank you body

(Inner eyebrow) For maintaining my ideal body weight

(Outer eye) I trust you body, to know what's best for our ideal weight

(Under eye) Thank you body, for maintaining our ideal body weight

(Under nose) You know better than weight charts and tables what's best for us

(Chin) Thank you body for maintaining my ideal body weight

(Collarbone) I love you body

(Under arm) I appreciate all that you do

Emotional health is all about learning to master your emotions. In order to do that, you've got to first begin to return to your authentic self. To rediscover your authentic self, you've got to begin to resolve trauma, release old hurts, release resentments, gain a new perspective, let go of the need to be right, learn to think in new ways, become aware of your emotional reactions to events and people and things that were said, and take full responsibility for your life and your actions.

Wow! That sounds like maturity, doesn't it? If you're like most people, you weren't taught these skills growing up. On the contrary, as I mentioned in the Physical Health section previously in this chapter, you were likely taught the opposite of these skills. They weren't modeled for you - not in your home life, not at school, not on TV, not in the movies, not in politics. But don't worry, it's not too late - no matter your current age. I've worked with women and men in their 80's. I've worked with children as young as 2. And every age in-between.

Emotional health means having emotional resiliency, which for most people, takes doing some inner work with a practitioner. Some people have emotional resiliency organically - they were nurtured and loved and cared for as they grew up. They have very little unresolved trauma. They felt secure in themselves, no matter what anyone else said. But that is more the exception than the rule.

Emotional health means not having to be right, even if you think you are right. This is huge and takes practice.

Emotional health requires taking good care of yourself - saying "no" when you mean no and "yes" when you mean yes. It means speaking your truth when it's appropriate to speak, and knowing when it's appropriate to not speak.

Emotional health calls for learning to forgive and apologize. I give lots of classes and workshops on forgiveness, and I've discovered that most people misunderstand what forgiveness is and what it means. If someone has done you wrong and needs to atone, forgiveness from your heart does not suggest that they no longer need to atone. Forgiveness doesn't mean you are letting them off the hook. It means you are letting *you* off the hook. You let go of holding on to whatever resentment you have towards them. Because that resentment is hurting you. Remember what I said in physical health - how your body responds to your mind? When we hold on to old hurts and anger, we are likely to create inflammation in our bodies. And most pain and many diseases are caused by inflammation - not the other way around.

I've also discovered that in many cases, people think they can't possibly forgive certain things. Let's say your ex-partner cheated on you. Could you forgive them? Most people tell me that they would be a fool to forgive. I say you'd be a fool not to forgive. Forgiveness, as I said, means letting yourself off the hook. You are not condoning what they did. But you are allowing yourself to be free of all that old toxic emotion.

You don't necessarily have to tell the other person that you've forgiven them. And you definitely don't need to invite them over for dinner! You don't need to email them or call them or text them, This forgiveness is energetic! It is mostly for your benefit.

If the act against you was more severe even than betrayal, you can still forgive. This may require outside assistance - like from a coach or spiritual advisor. It may require lots of prayer. But it can be done. Remember, you are letting yourself off the hook - releasing yourself from the responsibility of holding on to all the negativity. Below, there are two suggestions to move you toward forgiveness. It can't hurt you to try them.

When you take care of your emotional health, which will be a lifelong practice, the world is a better place. If by getting emotionally healthier, you are supportive of even one person, the world is better. If there is one less "I'm right, you're wrong" argument, the world is way better. If you come from a place of love and Grace in your dealings with the children in your life, the future will be better, too.

If you're waiting for the other person to apologize before you can forgive, think about that. They are much more likely to apologize if you've already forgiven them. That's an energetic response. If you're so pissed off at them and you are seething, they are not likely to come anywhere near you. But if you've let your hurt and anger go, if you've filled your heart with love, they will feel safer contacting you and being vulnerable. It's not a guarantee, but you will feel better, whether or not you get an apology.

And if you're saying to yourself, "There's no way I'm forgiving them! They owe me an apology! I'm not forgiving

until they apologize. Even then I might not forgive them!",
this is your ego talking. Your immature ego. And your immature ego will let you die before it allows you to change or
be vulnerable. So you've got to mature your ego in order to be
healthy. This takes patience and self-love.

Forgiveness isn't difficult. We just think it is. Forgiveness
begins with a decision to forgive.

Exercise for forgiveness.

This is a simple yet powerful exercise for forgiveness. If
you practice this for 14 consecutive days, it is likely you will
feel way less resentful toward the person or institution that
did you wrong. I want to reiterate that this does not free them
from atonement, amends, or reparations. Forgiveness is a decision you make, from your heart - to free yourself from any
further suffering.

For the next 14 days, pray (out loud if possible) for the
person or institution who has hurt you or harmed you. You
can pray to whatever deity or divine being you choose. This
can be God, Allah, Jesus, Angels, Universe, or whatever gives
you support. Your prayer can begin however you want, but
must contain a request for them (the other person or organization) to receive insight or healing for their greatest good.

So your prayer might go something like this:

"Dear Universe: I hope that Jason falls off a cliff while
he's hiking, but before he does, please help him to heal." Or;

"Dear God, you know I don't mean this, but I'm asking
you to heal Alana. And I wish for her all the good I wish for
myself." Or;

"Allah, please make Rabiya suffer as much as she made me
suffer. But also, show her your Divine love and compassion."

Keep praying for this person, day after day, every day for 14 days. Keep track so you don't stop short of that time period. Notice how you begin to feel by the end of the two weeks.

You see, praying for someone will help you verbalize how you really feel. As the days pass and you continue to pray for them, you will likely find your heart softening, and your words becoming less spiteful. Because as you say them out loud, you will realize that YOU really want to be happy, and that by holding on to these emotions, you are keeping yourself from happiness.

Tapping for emotional health and self-forgiveness.

It's always a good idea to forgive yourself first. Notice if you're feeling any guilt or blame for what happened. The following self-forgiveness Tapping protocol can be used easily throughout the day - for old and new resentments. Even when someone cuts you off on the freeway and you are angry, you can forgive yourself for holding on to that feeling, because it is hurting you more than it's hurting the other driver.

Tapping around the points, say one phrase at each Tapping point:

(Top of head) I'm so sorry, (fill in your own name here)
(Inner eyebrow) For thinking such hateful thoughts
(Outer eye) Please forgive me, (fill in your own name here)
(Under eye) For thinking/saying such hurtful things
(Under nose) Thank you for forgiving me, (fill in your own name here)
(Chin) I love you, (fill in your own name here)
(Collar bone) And I want the very best for you
(Under arm) I want the very best for you

This is one of the simplest and most powerful Tapping protocols ever. I've presented it in several places in this book It combines Tapping with the Hawaiian self-forgiveness technique called Ho'oponopono (ho-oh-po-no-po-no). I have seen clients have an enlightening experience by using this combination. By both asking yourself for forgiveness and giving yourself forgiveness, you have just stopped abandoning yourself, you've given yourself compassion and love, and you've touched your own Soul.

Tapping for forgiving them.

If you're finding it difficult to forgive them, try this Tapping protocol to see if you can loosen things up a bit. Don't force it, just tap and see what happens. Start by rating the intensity of your resentment, hurt, and anger towards the other person or institution. Use the 1-10 scale, where 10 is the most intense your feelings can be. Write down the number.

Tapping around the points, say one phrase at each Tapping point:

(Top of head) There is no way I'm going to forgive them for what they did
(Inner eyebrow) I could never do that
(Outer eye) I'm going to hold onto this hurt and anger
(Under eye) For as long as I possibly can
(Under nose) I'm not letting them off the hook!
(Chin) I'm not letting go of this hurt
(Collar bone) I may never let it go
(Under arm) I want to be sure everyone knows how hurt I am

(Top of head) Nope, I'm never letting this hurt go

(Inner eyebrow) It's keeping me safe
(Outer eye) People would think I don't care if I let this go
(Under eye) So I'm holding on to this hurt and anger
(Under nose) What they did was wrong
(Chin) And I want everyone to know that I know it
(Collar bone) I'm not letting go of this
(Under arm) I'm never letting go

Now take a deep breath. Sense into your resentment again. Think about the person or institution and what they did to you. Re-rate the intensity of your feelings, using the 1-10 scale. If the number went up from before, tap again, using this same protocol. It's actually a good thing when the number changes - even if it goes up. It means that energy is moving, shifting, and changing, and you're getting more in touch with your feelings. After another round or two of Tapping, notice your new intensity number. And if any new insights came up for you as you tapped, make a note of them and add them to your Daily Tapping list.

Remember, forgiveness seems difficult because we were never taught how to do it. But it really begins with a decision to forgive.

Please note: I am not a mental health provider. These comments and suggestions are not meant to replace your medical care, medications, or other mental health care. Mental health is derived from learning to notice your thoughts and beliefs. letting go of negative thoughts, releasing unreal thoughts (for example thoughts about the past or the future, or thoughts that assume things about what another person might be thinking or feeling, or why they acted a certain way)

Mental health in the context of this book is an integral part of all health. If you are thinking thoughts about yourself that are negative, untrue, and relentless, then you are beating yourself up, and are abandoning yourself. You may not even be aware that you're doing it. There's a good chance you weren't aware of how detrimental your own thinking has been to your well-being. When I work with groups, I often ask the participants what they say to themselves when they make a mistake or fail at something. Most people can easily access these thoughts. Some of the things people tell me they say to themselves are "Idiot!" "You're so stupid!" "You're just not good enough." "You'll never amount to anything." "You're such a disappointment." "God hates you." And worse.

Take a moment to notice the things you say to yourself when you're upset. Write them down now, or say them out loud.

Now imagine saying those things to a small child. Would you expect that child to thrive under those conditions? Then why would you say them to yourself? Do you expect yourself to thrive under those conditions? Or is this negative talk just an old habit? Maybe you're repeating what you heard as a child.

My personal experience with my own mental health is that for many years I did not attend to my mental health needs. All the years I drank alcoholically and was addicted to drugs I certainly didn't think in a sane manner. I didn't act in a sane manner. Not just according to society's definition of sane, but to my own definition. I did things that were wrong by my own standards and values. I felt out of control of myself and my own life. I was uncomfortable in my own skin and I did whatever I could to avoid feeling my own feelings. It wasn't until I got clean and sober that I began to have an inkling of how out of control I had been.

To this day, I give energy every day to noticing my thoughts and beliefs and improving my perspective and my-self. First getting sober and working the 12 Steps of Alcoholics Anonymous, then doing lots of Tapping, have given me the ability to do this self-work in a way I never could before. Like most things in this book, this is a lifelong practice.

For wonderful mental health, I recommend a daily medi-tation to quiet your mind. It can be as short as 3 or 4 min-utes. And then work your way up to longer periods of silence. There are lots of ways to meditate, and lots of books and apps available to help you. Quiet meditation is generally the most helpful, but if you prefer a guided meditation, that is a great place to start. Meditation isn't about stopping your thoughts. Meditation is about slowing your thoughts and simply observ-ing them - learning to let each thought go and not chase it. It's about learning how to wait, just wait, between thoughts, and to allow Divine inspiration to come in. You can pose a ques-tion before your meditation, and wait for a solution to arrive. Don't try to figure out the solution, just wait.

And of course, I recommend Tapping to clear your nega-tive emotions, interrupt your repetitive, habitual thought pat-terns, and to resolve your traumas so that you can actually quiet your mind. Tapping every day, throughout the day, is easy and powerful. Be kind and gentle with yourself. Love yourself. Care deeply for yourself.

All the Tapping in this book is in part to help you create better mental health. It's not about "fixing" you, because you don't need to be fixed. It's not about helping you become someone you're not, but rather, it's all about you becoming the most authentic version of you possible.

Learn to think for yourself. Be responsible for your thoughts. And reprogram your own mind to think like the person you really want to be. That's a great start to mental health! When you begin to manage your mental health, you can have a great impact on the people around you and around the globe!

Spiritual health. Often misunderstood, "spiritual" and "religious" are not necessarily interchangeable. Spirituality is not religion, although spirituality can be a part of religious practice. Being affiliated with a religion does not guarantee a spiritual practice. Your spiritual health includes caring for your Soul, practicing a connection with Divine Spirit/God, looking for your happiness within (not out there), and being of Service to others, with love and grace, not because you "should." Spirituality is also about raising your awareness and your consciousness.

I have met so many people who had too much religion as a child, or were stifled by the beliefs of their parents' church connection. They have moved away from religion, or denounced religion, and so, don't want to have anything to do with spirit or God. That is unfortunate. It is the ultimate in "throwing out the baby with the bathwater!"

Others have gone the route of Science vs. religion, and have decided it is one or the other. What if it can be both? What if the hard sciences are overlooking some important stuff, simply because it can't be seen or heard or tasted or touched. That would be like saying "I refuse to use the Internet because I can't see it." We don't see the Internet, we don't see gravity, we don't see energy. We only see the results of the Internet, gravity, energy. We have learned to work with those things for the benefit of Humanity.

Many other things also fall under the heading of spiritual practice and spiritual health. Forgiveness falls into the realm of spiritual health, but forgiveness also greatly affects your emotional, mental, and physical health. In fact, forgiveness just might be the single most powerful part of healing yourself and the planet. And since forgiveness is so misunderstood, I've included more detail about it earlier in this chapter.

In addition to forgiveness, there are several things that add to spiritual health that also add to emotional, mental, and physical health. For example, it's important for your happiness and spiritual health to sieve and sort out the positive fun memories from the negative ones. For instance, if you were in an intimate relationship with someone, and during that time the two of you had many wonderful experiences together. But then you or they decided to end the relationship because of some of the less wonderful things.

After you heal your hurt (see the earlier part of this chapter about forgiveness and self-forgiveness), it's best to sort and sift through your memories and release the negative ones and hold on to the positive ones. So many people do it the other way around - they can't seem to remember any positive memories, only the worst ones. It is really the ego that wants us to hold on to the hurts and let go of the loving feelings. We're afraid we'll want to get back together if we show love for them. Or we're afraid of what people might think if we have forgiven them. Or, quite simply, it feels too vulnerable. Remember what I said before about maturing your ego? This is another reason that is so important.

Once again, we are really hurting ourselves by releasing all the good stuff and holding all the negative stuff. When we do this, there is always something essential lost while getting rid of something unwanted. Another reason why we do that is to more easily cut psychic ties with others. In other words, it seems "easier" to break off a relationship if we're really angry, and if we stay angry. In the short term, it may be easier. But in the long term, it is way more difficult, uses a ton of energy, and harms us!

One of the side-effects of Tapping is a greater spiritual awareness and connection. I've worked with people of many different religions - Christian, Muslim, Jewish, Hindu - as well as spiritual with no religious affiliation, and agnostic. No matter their religious affiliation, Tapping helps them feel more whole and complete, more self-loving, more caring, more connected. These are symptoms of spiritual awareness. There is no divinity that I'm aware of that calls for us to hate ourselves or others. That is a human interpretation of religion and God!

Every interaction with another human is a chance to practice your spirituality, to raise your awareness and increase your consciousness. We are all connected. We all share the same emotions. We simply have different stories, different perspectives, different values, and different levels of understanding. When someone bugs you, it is because they reflect a part of yourself that you don't like, or possibly haven't accessed yet. The more you care for yourself, the more ready you will be to embrace that part of you. The more you love and accept yourself, the easier it will be for you to recognize our interconnectedness, and love and accept others. The more you realize that others aren't at the same place you are, the easier it will be to allow them to grow and evolve at their own pace. You can be an example for them, but it is highly unlikely that you will convince someone to grow spiritually.

It is in recognizing our interconnectedness that we can have the greatest impact on the world. In order to recognize our interconnectedness, we need to cultivate compassion. In order to cultivate compassion, we need to release old hurts and forgive. In order to release old hurts and forgive, we need to resolve our traumas and learn to love and accept ourselves. And that's why this book started with a chapter called "Stop Judging Yourself!"

[NOTE] There are times when a small amount of anger is a helpful emotion to get you moving in the right direction. If you are, for example, a woman in a relationship with an abusive man, you may need to find some anger in order to rally your resources. I'm not suggesting that you fight back with an abusive partner. Not at all. But in order to feel like you have a right to find help, you may need to get pissed. Always put your safety, and the safety of your children first. You know what's best!

That's what happened to me. I spent 10 years in a marriage with a man who verbally and emotionally abused me. At first, I didn't realize what was happening to me. He wasn't hitting me, so how could it be abuse? And when I finally made the decision and got the courage to file for divorce, I truly thought he might kill me. Obviously, he didn't. But I was lucky. If you are in such a relationship, carefully seek help. Don't endanger yourself or your children. [end note]

LEARNING TO MEDITATE

This is a starter tool for those who find meditation, or even the thought of meditation, more than they feel they can handle. Can you devote 3 minutes a day (or twice a day if you're motivated), for 30 days, to begin to experience some great results?

3 Minute Meditation.

Create a comfortable place, not on your bed, for meditation. This space should be quiet and a place where you can be free from interruptions from people, pets, outside noises. Eventually, you will hopefully be doing longer meditations, so make this your sacred space.

Bring your alarm or timer. Drink a glass of water before you begin, and take care of anything that can't wait 5 minutes.

Sit comfortably - on a chair or on the floor (use a mat or blanket). If you sit on a chair, keep your legs uncrossed, feet on the floor. Sit up, spine straight but not stiff, and make yourself as comfortable as possible. If you sit on the floor, you can put your legs straight out in front of you, or cross them in whatever manner is comfortable for you. Keep your spine straight but not stiff and feel your head as if it is floating, and yet firmly in place (not swinging around, though sometimes your head may "nod").

Relax your arms at your sides, resting your hands on your knees or thighs, fingers gently face upwards, to receive the energy.

Set your alarm or timer for 3 minutes. No more than that to start. You should always meditate for a little less time than you think is possible - so you always want more the next time. If you do this every day, there will come a day when you really look forward to it (if you don't already). Close your eyes, and breathe in gently through your nose, and exhale through your mouth. Begin to notice your thoughts. Just notice them. Don't judge them, or try to stop them. And don't hold on to them. Notice your thoughts as if you're standing at a bus stop. Each thought is a bus, and you're not going to get on any of them. You're just watching as one thought pulls up to the stop, and then pulls away. Let it go - don't chase it, don't even watch it as it pulls away. Then wait for the next one. It pulls up, and it pulls away. You don't get on. Breathe regularly throughout this meditation.

When your alarm goes off, turn it off, and remain in your seated position. Close your eyes again, and visualize yourself as the person you want to be - the person who makes the money you want to make, the person who speaks in front of large groups, the person who is in a loving relationship, the person who is authentic, calm and confident. The person who laughs easily and enjoys life without overdoing it. She challenges herself to be better and better, and encourages herself along the way. Whatever your picture for yourself is, visualize yourself there now. See yourself handling a tough situation, with grace and calm, and with a sense of lightness. Feel yourself doing the thing you want to do most - being the person you know you can be. Feel it as long as possible, then bring your hands to your heart as you end your meditation. Hold this feeling as you begin your day.

This is a great way to assist with creating new neuronal connections in your brain - new thought patterns that create new emotional patterns. You are on your way!

#9 TAKE 100% RESPONSIBILITY FOR YOUR OWN LIFE

"The more you take responsibility for your past and present, the more you are able to create the future you seek."

~Unknown

We live in a litigious society. Blame is everywhere. "It's your fault." "It's their fault." "It's all my fault." For most people, blame is a knee-jerk reaction. We're afraid of being blamed, so we blame others. We're afraid of what might happen, so we point the finger over there. We learned this behavior from our parents, from our peers, from our teachers, from television, from politicians and corporate leaders, from magazines and newspapers, and from electronic media.

But blaming others makes you the victim. It takes your power away. If someone slams into the back of your car, their insurance should pay for your repairs and your health care to get you back to "pre-wreck" condition. And if you live in the U.S., you may receive a settlement for your "pain and suffering." And that's ok. But if you continue to blame that driver for your ongoing problems, even your pain, you have relinquished your power. You have abandoned yourself. You have given your power away.

After all, you were driving too. You took a risk leaving the house. You took a risk getting into your car. It could have been you who made a mistake in judgment and hit the car in front of you.

Imagine a fender-bender in the parking lot at the neighborhood Whole Foods. Two drivers have both backed out of opposite parking spaces at the same time, and their cars have bumped into each other. Now imagine the driver of the first car getting out, pointing their finger and saying "it's all your fault!" In this scenario, the finger-pointing person has no power, no responsibility for anything, not even for being present. They have just said to the Universe "I'm powerless, I'm a victim." And guess what? The Universe will respond with more to feel powerless about, more to feel victimized about. Not because the Universe is vicious or wants to teach them a lesson, but because of the Law of Attraction. Whatever is our dominant energetic vibration is like a request to the Universe. And the Universe always says "yes!". It's time for this person to reclaim their personal power.

Imagine the other person being blamed for everything. It's likely their defenses will go up, and they will begin pointing their finger back saying, "No, it's your fault too!". And now the battle has begun.

Now imagine that same driver from the first car standing tall, voice strong, saying "We're both involved, and I'm sure we can resolve this." That says to the Universe "I'm powerful, I'm responsible, and I'm setting boundaries." Now they will begin to attract more to feel powerful and responsible about. The other person will likely feel less defensive, and be more willing to actually resolve the damages, even when they involve their insurance companies

Have you experienced something like the first scenario, where someone is blaming you for everything? How did you feel? Can you see how frightened the person must have been to act in that way? Or have you ever been the finger-pointer? Do you remember how frightened you were to cause you to act this way? In the case of the fender-bender, people often get instantly afraid of their insurance rates going up, their spouse being angry, getting in trouble with the police, lawsuits, and so on. Not to mention, now they're late for their appointment, they're going to have to deal with the inconvenience and expense of car repair, and on and on. The stress of it all can be overwhelming, and we often overreact.

But when we stop and breathe and tap, we can sort all that out, and get to what's really bothering us. We can be responsible for ourselves and our behavior, and demand others be responsible for themselves. And we can do it, usually, in a firm, kind way. That's empowerment. As soon as fear of the future or the past gets into this moment, we lose that power.

If you've been victimized as a child, it is logical and reasonable to blame your parents or caregivers, or the victimizer. When a child is victimized by his parent or grandparent or caregiver, the world becomes a confusing place. What situation can feel safe and secure when the very person who is supposed to protect you abuses you? But if you are now an adult, and you are still blaming your childhood abuser for your current state, I'm suggesting there is another way. A more empowering way. There is hope.

First, you'll need to resolve the old traumas. That is crucial. Find a competent, compassionate, experienced practitioner who knows how to truly resolve trauma, once and for all. Tapping is profoundly powerful for this, in the hands of such a practitioner.

Once all or most of the traumas are resolved, you can begin to take back your life and become your authentic self. Many people I know who suffered such traumas in childhood appear to be successful in the business world. But often they are holding on by a thread, trying to keep everything under control. They are not being themselves because they can't be. It has never felt safe, so they've learned other coping skills. These alternative coping skills eventually become too much to continue.

But I promise you, most people can recover, and if you're diligent, you can become your authentic, loving self. Possibly more authentic than you've ever been in this life!

If you feel that you need to continue to blame someone else for how your life is now, it may not be time yet for you to evolve and transform. That's ok. All in good time!

Can you begin to see how this Simple Step could have such a profound effect on the World?

You can't force others to take responsibility for their lives, but you can set the example. And you can stop taking responsibility for anyone else's life. Unless, of course, you are the caregiver or advocate for a baby or toddler, or elderly adult. If you can't be with that person 24/7, you simply can't be responsible for everything that happens to them. You have to take care of yourself. Do the best you can.

An exercise you can do right now.

Notice right now how this idea of taking 100% responsibility for your life is affecting you. Notice if any thoughts, sensations, memories, emotions, or arguments are coming up for you. Are you feeling uncomfortable? Is there a part of you that wants to say "But you don't understand!"? Do you feel a bit angry? Or a lot angry? Whatever you're feeling, it's totally okay. Make a note of it. Write it down.

Now, notice where in your body you're having the reaction. There is always a bodily sensation to go with our emotional reactions, even though we're not always aware of the sensation. If you can't seem to locate any sensations, don't worry. Just keep attempting to pay attention and notice. These exercises will help you become more aware of your bodily sensations, and that's a crucial step towards emotional resiliency. If you can, write down where you feel the sensation. How intense is it, on a scale of 1-10, with 10 being the most intense? Write the number down. Does this sensation have a voice? What is it saying? Write that down, too. Does this sensation make you want to run away? Or distract yourself with something else? Just notice it all. Write down what you can..

Now let's tap.

Tap on the side of the hand and say:

Even though I'm feeling this reaction, just reading about taking responsibility, I love and accept myself and my feelings. Even though my feelings are saying _____ to me (fill in with what the voice is saying), I love and accept myself and that voice

Even though I'm feeling this reaction at a 10 (or whatever your number is), I love and accept myself and these feelings. Now Tapping around the points, beginning at the top of the head, say one phrase at each point:

(Top of head) This reaction
(Inner eyebrow) -This reaction to taking responsibility for my life
(Outer eye) This sensation
(Under eye) I'm feeling this sensation in my _____
(Under nose) There's a voice that is saying _____
(Chin) -Just reading about Taking Responsibility for my life
(Collarbone) This reaction and this sensation
(Under arm) Reading about Taking Responsibility for my Life

(Top of head) I'm not going to take responsibility for my life!
(Inner eyebrow) This is a ridiculous idea!
(Outer eye) If I take responsibility for my life
(Under eye) And they don't take responsibility for theirs
(Under nose) I'll be screwed
(Chin) I'll be a doormat
(Collarbone) People will take advantage of me
(Under arm) I'm not doing it!

(Top of head) And you can't make me!
(Inner eyebrow) I'm not taking responsibility for my life!
(Outer eye) I'm a victim and I'm sticking to my story
(Under eye) I'm powerless, and I don't want to change
(Under nose) I'm not taking responsibility for my life!
(Chin) Someone else can do it
(Collarbone) I'm powerless

(Under arm) I refuse to take responsibility for my life!

Take a deep breath. Imagine taking responsibility for your life now. Is the reaction the same as before? Are the sensations the same? Check in with the sensations and attributes of it you wrote down before the Tapping. Rate the intensity of those sensations now. Has the number changed? Are the attributes the same or different?

Repeat this Tapping protocol up to 3 times, and whenever you need it. Notice what thoughts and ideas come up for you as you tap.

This topic can bring up a lot of feelings. Be kind and gentle with yourself as you work through this. I'm not suggesting that you tap until you agree with this idea of taking responsibility for your life. But rather, I'm suggesting that you tap until you clear your resistance to taking responsibility for your life. From that place, you can more clearly decide if you're ready for this or not. In other words, if you are resisting even the idea of taking responsibility for your life, you're not making a choice, you're simply reacting. But if you can clear the resistance, you can choose whether or not you want to take responsibility for your life - maybe now, maybe later - or if you want to continue being a victim. If you are simply reacting, there are old emotions driving your reaction. These old emotions need to be brought out into the light, aired out, and consciously dealt with. Sort of Emotional Spring Cleaning.

YOUR CHOCOLATE CAKE MOMENT

Taking responsibility for you life can be, for some, the most difficult thing you ever do. Especially if you've experienced a lot of hurt and abuse and trauma. If you think that life is unfair, or life is hard, it will seem unfair that you have to take responsibility for it. It will seem hard to do. In my many, many years of searching, the best reason I can think of for taking responsibility for my life, was the ultimate personal empowerment it confers. Accepting responsibility for my life means that I have the power to change my life. No one else does. I can't blame anyone for my life, or the events in my life. And I am responsible for my reaction or response to those events. After all, "It's not what happens to us in our lives, it's how we respond."

Ask yourself, "If I'm not responsible for my life, who is?" Ask yourself, "Am I expecting someone else to be responsible for me?" Do you want to be responsible for other people's lives? You can't. You simply can't be responsible for other people's lives. Unless, of course, that person is very young, or very, very old, or is disabled and in your care.

When you begin to take 100% responsibility for your life, life gets better. If you've never experienced this, imagine trying to explain chocolate cake to someone who's never had chocolate cake. Imagine that person having their first bite of chocolate cake - their taste buds are awakened, they smell the chocolate, every cell in their body does a happy dance. This is your chocolate cake moment. The joy of being responsible for your own life is beyond what you can currently imagine.

You have what it takes.

Taking 100% responsibility for your own life takes courage. It creates self-respect. It develops resourcefulness and character. If we don't take responsibility for our lives, we give our power over to others. We diminish ourselves. We abandon ourselves.

When I decided to take responsibility for my life, I was able to let go of responsibility for anyone else's life, including my kids. Of course, if they had been younger than 5, I would still have been responsible for their lives. But once they went off to Kindergarten, I realized that many other people would be influencing them and caring for them at least part of each day. And for the most part, I had no control over that. Of course I had some influence over who their teachers were, and I was an advocate for each of my kids. But I couldn't be with them every minute. Nor did I want to be the only influence in their lives. I didn't want to try to create "mini me's" I wanted each of my children to be an independent thinker, to learn to make healthy choices, to be resourceful. They couldn't have done that if I were hovering around them worrying all the time!

I decided early on to not worry about my kids when they weren't with me. No matter what. When they headed out of the house, I would say "Have fun!" or "Enjoy yourself," not "Be careful." Because I trusted them to make responsible choices. Even when I put my then 8-year-old daughter on a plane to visit her Gramma, I didn't worry. Once I put her on the plane, she was in the care of the flight attendants. And the pilot was flying the plane, not me. That daughter is now 27, living in Brooklyn and working in New York, and is responsible for her own life. She moved to New York several years ago, got a job and an apartment her first day there. That takes courage and character.

Later, when my second oldest daughter was 11, she was flying from Portland to the Big Island to visit her godparents. I took her to the airport early in the morning. When we checked in, we were informed that her flight was delayed by five hours. I had my own cafe at that time, and I simply couldn't take the day off to sit at the airport with her. I asked her what she wanted to do. She said I could take her home and she'd take the train back to the airport later. She got herself from our house to the train, to the airport, onto the plane, transferred planes in San Francisco, and arrived safely on the Big Island later that day. That daughter is now 25, is very independant, works in the Arctic region of Alaska, travels all over the world on her own. She is responsible for her own life.

Even my son - the youngest of my kids - learned responsibility early on. When he started third grade, he transferred to a magnet school located across town. I was rarely able to drive him to school, so he had to ride the city bus. This meant that he had to get himself to the bus stop on time, ride the bus, transfer to a second bus, and walk from the stop to school - all by 8:00 a.m. every day. He was never afraid, he had no problems getting to school that whole year. He is now 21 and lives on his own. He is responsible for himself and his own life. And he knows he can call me if he needs support or help. Or if he just wants to hang out with his mom!

I love my kids and care very deeply for them. But I don't worry about them. I would go crazy if I did. I raised them to be independent and responsible for themselves. I didn't do it perfectly, but I did it lovingly!!

Your Soul Has a Purpose!

Your Soul came here into this physical body at the time it did, in order to grow and expand its awareness and to learn something it needed to learn to return to wholeness, to return to where it came from (God). That is a tough concept to wrap your brain around sometimes. Like, "Why did my Soul need to experience that horrible thing? And what am I supposed to do with the experience?" When you can determine that these are not rhetorical questions, and take the time to investigate them further, you will gain some deep insights into the meaning of your life. You may need some outside help for this because you are so steeped in your own life.

Let's take those questions and dig a bit further now.

"Why did my Soul need to experience that horrible thing?" In order to answer that, you will need to resolve the trauma of the event. One of the most profound examples of why we sometimes need to experience horrible things, is from Project Light Rwanda. These young Rwandans were witness to genocide. Their parents were murdered. They experienced rape and other atrocities. And they survived. Then, they had to raise their surviving younger siblings, without any resources or assistance. And they still survived. With the help of Dr. Lori Leydon, they found healing, resolution, and *forgiveness*! Dr. Leydon used Tapping to help them heal.

And now these young people are helping others to heal. As "Ambassadors of Light," they share their experiences and healing, and show others how to heal - all over Africa, and the world. If *they* can find forgiveness for those who committed those atrocities, anyone can find forgiveness. Please note: their forgiveness does not mean they condone what was done to them or others. Forgiveness does not mean they think it was OK in any way. But they have resolved the trauma, and released the hurt from their minds and bodies. These young Rwandan ambassadors have inspired thousands of people to heal and forgive. They have gone on to university, which they wouldn't have been able to do if they were still experiencing their trauma. As of this writing, many of them have graduated from university, and have become school teachers, entrepreneurs, and heart-centered leaders,

There is one story in particular that always brings tears to my eyes and joy to my heart. Dr. Leydon was also called to Newtown, Connecticut in 2012, immediately following the shooting at Sandy Hook Elementary School, where 28 students and teachers were gunned down by a lone shooter. Dr. Leydon worked with the first responders and with the parents and the people of Sandy Hook, to help them resolve their trauma and grief. She and her team used Tapping.

In 2013, JT Lewis, the brother of one of the victims, was unwilling to return to school. Dr. Leydon spent time with him and wanted to introduce Tapping to him. He wasn't interested. Dr. Leydon had an inspiration. She set up a Skype call between JT and two of the Rwandan ambassadors. She did not prompt them, but because of their training as Ambassadors of Light, they shared their experiences and their healing, and they taught JT how to tap. The next day, JT returned to school. And in the next 60 days, he had raised enough money to send one of the Ambassadors to University and pay for food for her remaining family members for a year.

These are the miracles of healing!

If you are continuing the Trauma, rather than healing.

If you've been telling yourself and everyone else that you are a victim of childhood abuse, you are perpetuating the abuse. But the abuse is no longer actually happening to you. You are doing it to yourself. Ask yourself, "Who would I be if I hadn't been abused as a child?" Really pay attention to the answer you get. You can start becoming that now. By taking the steps outlined in this book. If you are blaming your lack of success, or your health issues, or your relationship problems, on your past, you are victimizing yourself. I know that's a lot to digest, so take it in small bites. Be gentle with yourself. Use the steps. Get assistance.

One day I suddenly asked myself why I wasn't taking responsibility for my life. Why was I still blaming my fears and lack of success on not receiving enough love and support as a child? That thinking kept me small. It kept me from moving forward. It created ongoing excuses for not doing and being all I was being called to do and be. I was victimizing myself.

I was 56 at that time. I asked the question that changed the course of my life in a big way. "Who would I be if I had been loved and supported?" In that moment I realized that I was still blaming the outcome of my life on my childhood experiences. It had been many, many years since I had emancipated. I was responsible for me. I was responsible for changing this old story, for letting go of something that only felt true, but wasn't really true. Whether it is true or not, it doesn't matter because it's not happening now, except in my head. And I'm the one perpetuating that event. In this moment.

And then I immediately got the inspiration to Tap and say "I've always known that I'm loved and supported." It was a profound moment. I tapped each of the Tapping points, repeating this phrase, even though a part of me wanted to not believe what I was saying. I realized that if I chose to and decided to, I could love and support myself - now, and in the future, and I could go back to the earliest version of me and love and support her. I knew, after all these years of Tapping, and after being sober for 25 years at the time, that I had always been loved and supported. Maybe not by my parents or family in the way I wanted, but certainly by God and angels.

Otherwise, I wouldn't be here. That part of me stopped arguing, and a huge old hurt was resolved in that moment. I have been moving forward in my life ever since.

What have you been telling yourself and others about why you haven't become the greater and greater version of yourself in all areas of your life? Have you been repeating that you were abused as a child or as a wife or partner? Have you been saying "That's just how we are in my family?" Are you ready to let loose of this old story and heal?

It might be helpful for you to know that the Universe doesn't do random acts of abuse. Everything happens so that your Soul can learn what it came here to learn. If not in this lifetime, it will try again in the next.

For a long time, I had a hard time believing that I was supposed to be someone who wasn't loved and supported as a child. But after 50 years, I finally realized that I was supposed to be someone who lived through that, healed, and then let go of the story that I wasn't loved and supported. Through the experiences of my life, I was given all the tools, skills, characteristics, experiences, inspiration, motivation, and circumstances to do just that. I lived through feeling not loved and not supported, had a 30-year history of feeling crappy about myself, living with trauma-related symptoms, working hard, trying to make people like me, abusing myself with drugs and alcohol, and on and on. Even after sobriety I felt so much shame and "not-enoughness." And now I've lived another 30 years. I am so grateful for Tapping for helping me to undo all that programming, and invite healing, awakening into my daily life.

Here's the Tapping protocol that helped rewrite my history, and it can help rewrite yours, too. I call these phrases "Preformations," because they are like affirmations, but they go back to the beginning and change things going forward.

Tapping around the points, use this phrase at the first and the final point, and fill in the other points with any combination of the other phrases. You can make up your own, starting with "I've always known that..." and fill in with the very thing you've been saying you didn't get. The fact that you know it's missing means you must have had it, at least a little bit. Otherwise, you wouldn't recognize it as missing.

(Top of the head): I've always known that I'm loved and supported
(Inner eyebrow): I've always known that I'm powerful
(Outer eye): I've always known that I can trust my intuition
(Under eye): I've always known that I am wise
(Under nose): I've always known that it's safe to speak my truth
(Chin): I've always known that I'm amazing and unique
(Collarbone): I've always known that I can choose my own beliefs
(Under arm): I've always known that I'm loved and supported

Take a deep breath. Notice if any of these phrases triggered a response of "That's not true," or some other resistance. The fact is, if you feel as though you weren't loved and supported, it's usually because you were counting on your parents or caregivers to do the loving and supporting. There's a good chance they couldn't love and support you like you wanted. Likely, they hadn't felt loved and supported themselves. But truly, they did the best they could with the resources and knowledge they had at the time. They loved you the best they could. And the fact is, you were loved and supported by the Universe. Just as I was. And as every person is. You just didn't realize it. But it's not too late to realize it now. You can start to love yourself now. It's never too late to love yourself now and then. See chapter one.

The same is true for any other statement that you make about yourself. Even if you didn't feel safe to speak your truth, you really did have access to God, the All-Knowing. You just weren't aware of it. And I can promise you, the Universe/God/Divine Spirit Mother or Father/Allah really did have your back. But you needed to have the experience of feeling utterly powerless in order to find your power. You needed to feel as though you weren't loved and supported in order to discover what real love and support is. You've needed to go through everything you've gone through to learn what you need to learn. Life isn't pointless!

And if you're not ready to learn yet, you may need to go through some more stuff around the issue. Life is a process of "uncover, discover, discard." Uncover the issue, discover your responsibility for your current state and learn what you came to learn, and discard the things (the thoughts, beliefs, relationships and the stuff) that aren't serving you any longer.

When you get clarity and balance in one issue or one area of your life, you will uncover another one. If you've ever been in the ocean, waiting for the next wave, you get a sense of this process. When I was a kid, I lived in Hawaii, where I did a lot of bodysurfing with my friends. We would swim out just past where the waves started to break, and then we'd wait. There was no point in taking a "junk" wave, or in trying to start paddling before the wave arrived. You just had to wait, bobbing around in the water. And then a really great wave would finally appear. If you were in tune with the ocean, you would start to paddle and catch the wave. The ride might be a rush where you got into the curl of the wave and rode it out to its completion. Some waves might not be too exciting. The ocean might dump you onto the sand, or swirl you around and upside down. But it was all good. It was all for the love of bodysurfing.

Life is like that. Do you love life and enjoy waiting for the waves and riding them? Do you appreciate the joy of Life? Or do you only enjoy the "perfect wave?'

Even when you get the hang of it, there will be times when you will enjoy the "uncover, discover, discard" process, and there will be times when you feel like "What the hell? Is this ever going to end?" A shift in perspective can change every-thing! I encourage you to stay curious. Keep moving forward. Keep looking inward for your solutions. Keep Tapping to help you get resiliency and awakenings. Life is a journey, not a destination. Learn to enjoy the journey.

#10 KNOW YOUR VALUES...
AND YOUR VALUE!

"Something I just recently learned is that chased love is not love. If you have to run after it, talk it into staying, remind it of your value, fight alone for the both of you, issue ultimatums, or test it - it is not love! It's not love, it's not happiness, it's not fair, it's not healthy. The only thing it is is a waste of your time."

~Jessica James

What are personal values and how do they affect your value?

I love this definition: "Your personal values are a central part of who you are – and who you want to be. By becoming more aware of these important factors in your life, you can use them as a guide to make the best choice in any situation. Some of life's decisions are really about determining what you value most."

I realize that there are probably lots of different ways of interpreting personal values and I could probably write a whole book on that. But for this book, I'm going to use my interpretation of values. You are free to interpret it however you like. Remember, we are learning ways to have a profound impact on the world, not to argue with each other. So keep an open mind, take what works for you, and leave what doesn't.

In essence, personal values are the things, the actions, the beliefs that are truly important to an individual. Our values represent what we are for, not what we're against. For example, you may value justice. And this value may be important to you because of injustice in the world, or perhaps injustices that have happened to you. You are against injustice, and for justice. We can often determine our values by noting what we're against, and then turning that around to state what we're for.

"Personal values" can be an emotional topic because not everyone knows their own values, and quite frankly, most people are out of integrity with their values. Not intentionally, but because they haven't identified their personal values and committed to them. Everyone is entitled to their own set of personal values, and everyone is where they are in their awareness. Let's do some Tapping on the general emotions around personal values.

Notice how you feel when you think about someone who acts in a way that goes against something that is important to you. If you value responsibility, and someone in your life is acting irresponsibly (by your estimation), what name do you give the emotion or emotions that come up for you when you imagine or remember a scene like this? Write those down. Where do you feel those emotions in your body? Write that down, too. How intense is the sensation or your reaction to someone else acting against your values?

Tapping on the side of your hand, say these phrases:

Even though I have this feeling when I think about someone acting in opposition to my values, I deeply and completely love and accept myself

Even though it stirs up [name of emotion you wrote down], I deeply and completely love and accept myself

Even though I wish other people would respect my values, I love and accept myself, and I CHOOSE to feel peaceful, even if it's just while I'm doing this tapping. A little peace. A lot of peace. It all begins with me.

Now Tapping through the points, say one phrase at each point:

(Top of head) This feeling
(Inner eyebrow) This emotion
(Outer eye) My values are important to me
(Under eye) It bothers me when others don't act in accordance with my values
(Under nose) I wish people would understand my values
(Chin) And respect my values
(Collarbone) Like I understand their values
(Under arm) And respect their values

(Top of head) My values are important to me
(Inner eyebrow) Their values are important to them
(Outer eye) Our values don't always match up
(Under eye) And it bothers me
(Under nose) I think people should be more like me
(Chin) I think my values are right and theirs are wrong
(Collarbone) I wonder if they think the same thing?
(Under arm) I wonder if tolerance is one of my values?

Take a deep breath. Drink some water. Check back in with the feeling you wrote down. Do you still feel overwhelmed (or whatever your feeling was)? It's okay if you do, it's okay if you don't. Just notice again.

If you still feel that feeling, is it in the same place (head, chest, stomach, or wherever)?

Re-rate the intensity of whatever the feeling is or was. Write down the new number. There are no right or wrongs in this protocol. You are entitled to whatever feelings and emotions you are having. Jot down the new number, and notes about anything else that came up for you during the round. Any insights? New emotions? All feelings and emotions are for our benefit. We just need to learn to listen to them.

GETTING CLARITY

Most of us think we know what's important to us, but most of us haven't gotten really clear about our personal values. Most of us haven't made a commitment to live by our values. In order to create a life that feels rich and fulfilling, it's important to get clarity about your values so that you can create boundaries for your decisions and actions. Without these boundaries, your life may feel like it would to take a road trip across the U.S. and take every side road you come to. It's fun to take a side road when you choose it, but you probably don't want to take them all!

As you gain clarity about your Personal Values, I encourage you to consider where you prioritize COURAGE, LOVE, & INTEGRITY. These three are valuable wayposts on your life journey. It takes courage to live by your values. Are you up for the challenge of living a valuable life? Are you interested in increasing your own value? If not, you can develop courage. Make it a higher priority, and it will naturally develop when you give it your attention and intention. Love is the force that keeps us alive, keeps the Earth spinning on its axis. If you want to end hate in the world, if you want to heal, make Love a priority. Live your life, make your choices, speak your words, take actions from a place of Love. Love is the antidote to fear. Again, if love isn't a top-10 value for you, consider moving it up your list. "Integrity is required to live by your values. it's important to discover how important integrity is to you. This can also be developed. You certainly don't have to prioritize courage, love, and integrity right now. But if not now, when?

As you go through this process of discovering your personal values, ask yourself which of these values you are willing to stand up for. For example, if love is one of your top values, are you willing to stand up for love? Do you have the courage to respond with love when you see hate or fear? If not, that's okay. But take a deeper look at how important the value of love is to you. If you have a value with an exemption, (for example "Love...but only for people I love"), own it. Then you can do the work to more fully integrate the value into your actions and words so that it has no exemptions. Because you see, personal values with exemptions aren't our goal. Living in integrity with our values is our goal.

When we get clear on our values and get clear about how important our values are to us, we begin to value ourselves more. When we live our values, we gain self-esteem, self-respect, and the esteem and respect of others. Not everyone will respect us when we live our values, so it's essential to your well-being to determine how important it is that everyone agrees with you.

It's essential to determine where courage falls on your priority list, if at all. Because it takes courage to live by your values. It's totally okay if your top-priority personal value is, for example, "fitting in." I think the important thing is to get clear for yourself. This clarity can guide your decisions and behavior and can eliminate regret, thus increasing your own self-worth. This is called integrity, authenticity, honesty.

Personal values are not just a list of words. They are not nebulous ideas. Personal values are the architecture and the framework of your life. If you're clear on your values and living from those values, the structure of your life will be strong and influential. But when you are not clear on your values, or are living out of integrity with your values, your life's structure will feel flimsy. Therefore, when we take a good look at our values, we can begin to discover where we are living out of alignment, creating a rickety structure. And from there, we can begin to make subtle and not-so-subtle changes in our thoughts and actions that will have us living more in integrity with who we truly are. We can influence others by our actions when our own framework and architecture is firm and cohesive. This does not imply convincing others or coercing others, but rather respecting others, and having them respect us.

Values that are out of alignment.

Let's look closer at an example of values that are out of alignment. One of my personal top 5 values is "compassion." This has not always been one of my top values. In fact, when I was a child and an adolescent, I don't think I was very compassionate at all. Not to others, and not to myself. But as I've grown and changed and done a lot of inner work, my capacity for compassion for myself and others has increased tremendously. But there are times when I find myself judging someone for their actions, even though I teach others about why people act the way they do. When I catch myself, I can awaken my compassion, and let go of the judgment. One of the great things about doing this work is that I recognize that I no longer need to be perfect at something, that I am always making progress.

Here's something to consider. When you know your values and live by your values, you will begin to value yourself more. And other people will value you more. And the corollary is also true: when you value yourself, it's much easier to live your values and other people will value you too. This is where integrity resides!

Most people have only a vague idea of what their values are, and so they don't really know what to stand up for and what isn't important to them. This makes it easy for others to influence them. It makes the structure of their life rickety. But once we get clarity that one of our values, for example, is "respecting human life," we can gain clarity about what we support and don't support, when we speak up and how we speak up. It's out of alignment to kill to support our value of "respecting human life." It's difficult to value ourselves when we are out of alignment. Most people I work with don't value themselves. As they begin to value themselves, they feel like they deserve to live their values. This is the opposite of a vicious cycle - it is a compassionate cycle. Instead of ripping us apart, it creates an upward, outward expansion.

Why aren't we taught to determine our own values, to decide what's important to us? Why aren't we taught to value ourselves and others? In great part, it's because the people who came before us thought we should have *their* values.

They weren't clear about their values, and often, they didn't value themselves and others.

This is particularly noticeable in families, tribes, cultures, ethnic groups, and religions, where large groups of people are pressured and coerced and shamed into being and thinking a certain way. These are non-loving approaches and have a profoundly negative effect on Humanity.

ORGANIZATIONAL VALUES

Businesses and organizations also benefit from a clearly defined, clearly communicated set of values. A well-run, sustainable business is clear about its values and communicates those values to its employees, its board, and its customers. And it values its people and the planet along with its profits. Ideally, all decisions made on behalf of the company, all actions taken by its employees and board, align to those values.

Imagine going to work, whether you work for yourself or someone else, and being clear on your company's values. Imagine having the authority to make decisions and take actions in alignment with those values. So, for example, you work as a department buyer for The Whole House Hardware Company, in their main retail store. WHHC's values are: Satisfied customers is our number one goal. We treat our employees with respect. We are a sustainable company. The tagline for WHHC is: Healthy, Happy People on a Healthy, Happy Planet helping you create a Healthy, Happy Home.

As a Buyer for the company you can make decisions within the framework of those values. These guidelines tell you how to treat your customers and your employees, and also remind you that you need to help the company generate a profit. All in a framework that is clearly communicated and concise.

You can delegate to your employees by giving them responsibilities and reiterating the company's values. Make decisions and take actions within the values.

More on your personal values.

For more fulfillment in your life, more happiness, and less wasted time, it is important to gain clarity about your values. Like a well-run business, you will begin making decisions and taking actions that align with your values. It's going to make most parts of your life soooo much easier! Imagine having specific guidelines for your activities, for your work, for how you spend your time and your money. If you've ever felt like you have little self-control, this is going to help a lot!

The more you can think, act, and respond through the filter of your own personal values, the happier you will be. The one provision is that you determine your own values for yourself. Don't just take on other people's values out of habit or out of family loyalty (unless, of course, family loyalty is your top-rated personal value!)

Let's do a couple of exercises to help you determine your values, and to pare them down to your top 4-7. Your values can, but don't have to, match your family's values. Or your cultures. Or your religion's. At work, you don't have to have the same values as the company you work for. For happiness sake, at least some of your values should align with your employer's.

After you do the exercises in this chapter and have determined your personal values, I recommend you write them down on a note card and carry them with you. Put them on sticky notes around your office space and home. Reflect on them regularly. It's very easy to move away from our values and make excuses for not acting in accordance with them. When we do that, we naturally value ourselves less. When we value ourselves less, we value others less. There's that vicious cycle.

Values describe personal standards of what is valuable or important. This is what we're focusing on in this chapter, although our personal values will be influenced by our ethical and moral leanings.

My personal values are important to me, but I need to consider that your personal values are equally as important to you. And neither of us has the right to impose our personal values on each other, the community, or the collective. It is imperative that we learn to honor our own values and honor others' values as well. There are times when it is imperative that we find our courage and stand up for our values. This may feel frightening. Only you can decide when to do this.

Note: If you're running your own business, your personal values will likely be reflected in your company's values. The smaller your business, the more like you it will likely be. In other words, your business is a reflection of you. Or at least it ought to be for your greatest success and enjoyment. As your business grows, your company's values may expand to include new values. For greatest overall success, you will need to align with your company's values. For greatest overall success, you will need to align with your company's values.

EXERCISES FOR DETERMINING YOUR PERSONAL VALUES

Exercise #1 use the list.

Here is an extensive list of core values. I'm sure there are more values, which you can add if you want. Read through the list and cross off any values that are clearly not a high priority for you. Read through the list again and, circle any that feel like "Top-10" values. These feel really important to you.

Count how many you circled. If more than 10, you need to go through again. Get the list down to 10 or less.

CORE VALUES LIST:

Authenticity	Determination	Learning
Achievement	Education	**Love**
Adventure	Fairness	Loyalty
Authority	Faith	Meaningful Work
Autonomy	Fame	Money
Balance	Friendships	Motivation
Beauty	Fun	Openness
Boldness	Growth	Open-mindedness
Compassion	Happiness	Optimism
Challenge	Hard work	Patriotism
Citizenship	Health & Fitness	Passion
Commitment	Honesty	Peace
Community	Humor	Perseverance
Compassion	Influence	Pleasure
Competency	Inner Harmony	Poise
Consistency	Innovation	Popularity
Contribution	**Integrity**	Positivity
Courage	Justice	Recognition
Creativity	Kindness	Reliability
Curiosity	Knowledge	Religion
Dependability	Leadership	Reputation

Respect	Service to Others	Status
Responsibility	Spirituality	Trustworthiness
Security	Stability	Wealth
Self-Respec	Success	

Take your Top 10 Values and write them down. Number them from 1-10, in order of personal importance to you. Keep at it until you feel good about your priorities. Now take your top 5 and ask yourself the following for each one:

- Is this truly important to me?
- Does this value conflict with any others on my Top 5 list?
- Do I currently live as if this value is important to me?
- If no, in what areas of my life do I veer from this value?
- Am I willing to make decisions and take actions that reflect this value?
- Am I willing to treat others as I would like to be treated?
- Do I treat myself as if I believe in this value?
- Can I accept that others may not value this as I do?

If you answered no to any of these questions, notice how that feels. It is an opportunity for you to take a look at your life and yourself and to grow. It is helpful to come from a place of love when doing this values work, rather than judgement or "shoulds." You don't have to share this list with anyone else.

Exercise #2 life experiences.

Think back over your life and identify some of the times you felt:

- Really, really happy and satisfied. What was happening? Who were you with? What other factors played into your feelings. Write these down. These are your values, or clues to your values.
- Proud of yourself or someone else. What was the situation? Who was there? Write these down. These are your values, or clues to your values.
- Deeply fulfilled. What did that feel like? What was happening? Who was there. Write these down. More clues to your values.

Are you seeing some themes? Are family members involved? Is work involved? Do you get recognition? Are you sharing these experiences with others? Are you feeling connected? Are you making money? Are you in nature?
From this, you can determine your most important values. Narrow your list to your Top 5

Exercise #3 end-of-life visualization.

I went to workshop once where this exercise was given. I found it powerful.

Visualize the end of your life. You are not ill, but it's time to die peacefully. You have said goodbye to loved ones and friends. You have lived a long life. As you see yourself there, resting peacefully, ask your end-of-life self these questions, and capture the answers:

- What are you grateful for?
- What are you proudest of?
- What do you wish you'd done more of?
- What do you wish you'd done less of?
- What can you see now that isn't nearly as important as you thought it was?

- Who are the important people in your life - now and in the past?
- Is there any way you could have done that relationship better?
- This exercise will help you further identify your values by taking you into the future.

There are many possible ways to determine your core values. If these exercises haven't worked for you, I hope you will continue to find ways to discover what is most important to you. By determining your core values and living by them, you will have the greatest impact on the world!

Exercise #4 take your newly identified values out for a spin.

Write your 5 top values on a note card. Look at the card each morning and throughout the day. Don't just look at the card, read the words and really feel into them. Are these values how you want to live your life? Do they reflect who you really truly are? Are these values authentic for you?

Now spend a few days with them. How much are these values already a part of your life? Are there situations where you quickly or easily shun your own values? At first, you may need to adjust your values priorities a bit. But then it is important to not waffle. Over time, we grow and change. So every year or so, re-visit these exercises to give your values an update. How does that feel? How could you change the situation or change your value? Take more time if needed to come up with a Top 5 list of personal values that resonates with you. Then choose to adopt these values and live them consciously. Notice what happens in your life as you do.

You are a magnificent, powerful, unique child of God. Do what you need to do to discover your true self and your gifts. Love yourself. Find your personal power. Enjoy your life! Love others and don't hesitate to tell them. Appreciate what you have. Give gratitude. You are blessed!

Upon closing, I'd like to leave you with this quote from Richard Rohr, Franciscan Monk.

"God resists our evil and conquers it with good, or how could God ask the same of us? Think about that. God shocks and stuns us into love. God does not love us if we change; God loves us so that we can change. Only love—not duress, guilt, any form of shunning, or social pressure—effects true inner transformation."

MAY YOU FIND DEEP ABIDING INNER-PEACE AND SHARE IT WITH THE WORLD

Helen

ABOUT THE AUTHOR

Every person has a genius within, and every person has a True Life Purpose. Helen McConnell can help you unearth both. She believes that if every person began to tap into even 1% more of their potential, the world would be transformed. She's on a mission to make that happen.

Helen is a Personal Transformation Specialist. She works with individuals and organizations to maximize the sustainable creative potential of the Human Resource, by teaching the Art and Science of Mastering Your Mind.

Helen has studied the human psyche and human behavior for over 25 years. She is a Certified EFT/Meridian Tapping Practitioner, and is an expert in Clinical and Advanced EFT techniques. She also uses NLP, hypnosis, personal energy profiling, creative visualization and more.

Visit Helen at HelenMcConnel.com or email her at Helen@HelenMcConnell.com

Made in the USA
San Bernardino, CA
10 July 2018